FAITHFUL HEARTS

Essays and Poems Celebrating People's Relationships
with Their Pets

THE WRITERS' CACHE

Faithful Hearts: Essays and Poems Celebrating People's Relationships with Their Pets

Copyright © 2024 by The Writers' Cache

All rights reserved. The contributors retains all rights to his/her work. No part of this publication may be reproduced, distributed, or transmitted in any form or by any means, including photocopying, recording, or other electronic or mechanical methods, without the prior written permission of the contributor, except in the case of brief quotations embodied in critical reviews and certain other noncommercial uses permitted by copyright law.

ISBN: 978-1-7360125-8-1

Cover design © The Writers' Cache based on *A Special Pleader* by Charles Burton Barber, back image *Cats by a Fishbowl* by Horatio Henry Couldery

Contents

1. Teton — 1
   Fawn Groves
2. Faithful Heart: Aura — 9
   Dianne Hardy
3. My Cat Has No Good Manners — 20
   LaVern Spencer McCarthy
4. Trash Can Tyrant — 22
   Woodrow Walters
5. Horse Girl — 26
   E.B. Wheeler
6. Homing Instinct — 33
   Sharolyn Richards
7. Live Streaming — 39
   John Savoie
8. A Tale of Tails: How I (Almost) Overcame My Canine Phobia — 40
   Edmond Porter
9. Lady Meow — 48
   Michael Oborn
10. Geronimo! — 52
    Sherrie Gavin
11. Old Dog at Night — 71
    John Savoie
12. The Gift — 73
    Tim Keller
13. Pets Are for Kids — 84
    David S. Taylor
14. When It Rains in Spain — 94
    Anne Stark
15. Up A Tree — 102
    LaVern Spencer McCarthy

16. Marry a Cat Man — 103
McKel Jensen

17. The Marrow of the Matter — 116
Felicia Rose

About the Authors — 123

ONE

Teton

FAWN GROVES

Part One: Promises

If a fortune teller had told me five years ago that, in five years' time, I would be writing an essay about my dog, I'd have asked for my money back. It's not that I was a callous person; I just didn't see a dog in my future—mainly because I didn't want a dog in my future.

I grew up with family dogs, who were nice, but inconvenient. In my featherweight childhood years, our ambling Labrador retriever routinely left me face down and stupefied in his wake. During my image-conscious teen years, our shepherd mix imposed a wardrobe's worth of clinging hair, as persistent and unwelcome as acne. And as I visited home from college for rushed weekends of free laundry and home cooking, my shepherd guilted me with slobbery fetch toys and a hopeful underbelly. "Please? Just one scratch or gooey game of fetch before you drive away?"

So, a tidy adulthood without a dog suited me fine.

Unfortunately, a dogless life didn't particularly suit my partner. She wanted a running companion and a camping buddy, a late-night protector and a movie-night pillow. For a while, I won the disagreement, but after she singlehandedly maintained our household while I vanished into three years of graduate school, I thought the least I could do was surrender my stronghold.

I had hardly uttered my change of heart before she was online in a flurry of searching, looking at every available golden retriever across the Mountain West. I tried to conceal my rising fear of the unknown as she showed me photo after photo of—I swear—the same dog.

I told her I would take care of any dog she chose, and I meant it. I would let the dog live inside, fill its food and water bowls when low, and even take it for the one or two walks around the block that it would surely need each week. After all, I am a humanitarian.

My partner found a shelter called Companion Golden Retriever Rescue, CGRR, and was ready for me to meet the dog that she insisted "chose her." She asked whether I wanted to pick him up on Saturday or Sunday. That was a no-brainer—Sunday, of course. Why would I own a dog for an extra day? So, Sunday it was. We hopped in the car and headed to South Jordan, but not before stopping to buy a dog book for the drive.

The drive from Logan to South Jordan takes just under two hours. I learned on that January day that two hours is just enough time for an otherwise optimistic person to grow fully terrified of dog ownership. Dogs need *meals*? What ever happened to loading up the bowl and refilling when empty? Dogs have to walk every *day*?? For an *HOUR*?? Who was this Dog Whisperer anyway? But there was no turning back now. All I could do was put on my best smile for the nice people at the rescue.

I had to admit that Teton, as we called him, was quite beautiful. He was horribly undernourished and his ribs showed through, but he was happy and loving. After some walking practice with the trainer, and multiple reminders that I should look ahead at the sidewalk and not down at the dog, the managers entrusted us with our new boy. We loaded him up and as we pulled away into the crisp morning, I was encouraged by the fact that the event had gone smoothly.

Sixty seconds later...

As my partner turned through the first intersection leaving the rescue, I heard a small whimper and a not-small commotion over my shoulder. I shifted in my seat, just in time to see all 70 pounds of Teton scramble from the hatchback over the back seat and into my lap to tell me personally that he would have a lifetime fear of car travel. That's good information to know before beginning a two-hour drive at freeway speeds and through a canyon to boot.

I spent the rest of the ride on my knees in the back seat playing linebacker with my new dog and sending mental tweets to Mr. Dog Whisperer about what a *crock* the magic of his calm-assertive energy was.

But what a difference a dog makes. I don't remember if one day passed, or two, before Teton made his first of many moves into my heart. CGRR management had suggested that we keep him on leash, even in the house, for his first few days with us. So, tied to my waist, Teton shuffled with me from room to room, patiently waiting for me to decide where we'd go next. After following me in the kitchen from stove to sink to fridge to kitchen table, I took a seat and looked over at this dog, who was coming to a sit beside me, not sure how much rest he could count on. As his thoughtful eyes met mine, all in a moment, I could read him. He seemed to say, "I'm not really sure what's going on and I'm a little scared, but I'm going to try my best for you, and I hope I make you happy." In that moment, something shifted and I felt a fundamental softening in my core. I came to an instant understanding that this dog—my dog—had a soul.

I answered him, also with my eyes. I said, "I also don't really know what's going on, and I'm a little scared, but I promise you my very best, and I hope I make you happy, too." Today, almost five years later, as I write this essay with Teton at my feet, I'd say we've both made good on our promises.

Part Two: Seven Thousand Walks

If a sage had shown me ten years ago how, in ten years' time, Teton would slip from this world, leaving me in a well of grief and memories, I would have seized the privilege a thousand times. Those years ago, amid the harried pace of my important world, full of speed walking, speed talking, multitasking, rushing everywhere to arrive after everything has begun, to return home after all has been put away... I would have paused. I would have held it all at bay for ten years with Teton.

My wife and I called him our time vacuum. He certainly didn't arrive on the scene with a satchel full of spare minutes on offer. Instead, he instantly required time—lots of it, for walking and feeding and training and bathing and playing and scooping and scratching just the right spot. But something about making Teton happy made me happy and, in spite of the time required, it felt like a square trade.

For his part, Teton traded in units of pressure, leaning in hard to tell me, *You're my person.* He traded in silly entertainment, romping with gangly, giddy abandon, and in grateful indulgence, devouring a birthday or Christmas meal with something delectable drizzled on top. Watching Teton lap up whatever was good in life made me smile for having offered it.

And while Teton enjoyed a thing, it was the *only* thing. Life was only delicious. Whether the day offered a belly-deep wade in a sleepy backyard canal, a scrum at the dog park, or just an old, stuffed penguin, life was as good as it needed to be. Joy was as simple as carrying Saturday's mail inside, straight from the postman's hand. The right-now was as delectable as a not-quite-empty yogurt cup, the appearance of which reliably sent Teton into frenzied offering. *Mom! I'm sitting! I can lay down! Roll over!! Shake? Sit harder? Shake with <u>this</u> hand?! Back to <u>THIS</u> one?! Pleeease, give me that dairy goodness!!*

Then, watching Teton's whole body smile as his world fit into a plastic cup made me smile, too. Teton taught me that contentment is always within arm's reach. If you don't catch it with one hand, find it with the other. And, even when your cup is mostly empty, always smile thank you.

Tonight, as the sun fades, I sit in Teton's absence, instinctively fidgeting toward his evening walk. It is the hour when, always, I am too busy and too settled, with too much work on my lap, all too pressing to set aside. Teton waits patiently, optimistically, for me to lay down job things and pick up dog things for his second daily walk. One "Just a minute" at a time, I could drain away the evening's minutes, along with his golden anticipation. So, as if to save us both from my overcommitted day, he rests his chin on my keyboard, gently and persistently, to tell me what is more important. There's a world out there. It's time to be in it.

His humility, his canine wisdom, and those eyes—his deep, auburn gaze that seized me all at once ten years ago—pulls me to my feet every time. Amid the day's grasping expectations, Teton and I carve time to venture outside. We choose left or right, mountains or schoolyard, or simply all the smelly shrubs between home and dry cleaner. It doesn't really matter. Right now, today's walk is the only thing. Come sunshine, blustery snow, muddy rain puddles, or pressures of the world bearing down, Teton taught that there is always time to walk.

As we walked, twice each day, every day, through ten years' time, we witnessed ten autumns drain away ten summers' green and reinfuse the mountainside with explosions of red, yellow, and orange. And then, one golden sunset at a time, we witnessed autumn's palette cool into winter's white hush. As the world exhaled into blanketed rest, Teton inhaled it all, dashing and burrowing in powdered snowscapes, then falling in at my side, the cadence of our six footprints crunching against snowy solitude.

Just in time, as winter's gray freeze began to chill the bones, a sleepy spring inhaled, and tight-fisted buds on waking branches stretched their fingers to offer new life. In the glistening thaw, Teton darted from nook to hollow to crevice, chasing his nose in urgent discovery, tracking fresh scents and unearthing new treasures. "Just exquisite! So splendid!" he would wag.

And even when spring's fresh cool folded to summer's punishing heat, we walked. Teton showed me that there is time to follow a trail where it leads and that, sometimes, on the other side, beyond climbing and bushwhacking, rubbing at scrapes and stings, we are greeted only by a decaying carcass, stinking and teeming and stiff. And still, Teton taught, this calls for gratitude, too. "Just look what I've *found*!" Teton would wag, "Isn't it smelly and bloated and *fantastic*?!"

Somehow, he is right. In spite of the stinking offense, over my shoulder opens a mountain panorama unlike any possible from below. Here is pure perspective, brilliant bloom, and silence. Deadlines and devices are a world away.

Ten years ago, I wondered why I would own a dog for an extra day. I know now. A single day offers up as much life as I will live. The day is an unassuming bud on an outstretched branch, just above my gaze. Its gift inside, large or small, vibrant or common, will unfold, whether I pause to witness or not, render its joy or not, share it with others, or not. Today invites us to live in its moments, not beneath its minutes; to shed frenzy and share connection. Today invites me to inhale, and even when stink and carcass seem closest at hand, a full-color panorama lies just beyond.

Tonight, my heart and home feel hollow without Teton by my side. I miss the *scritch-scratch* of his steps as he approaches and settles into me. I miss the rise and fall of his breath and his warmth on my fingertips. But Teton taught that in the cold and the gray, simply enough, we must walk. And just now, it is time. So instead of my coat, I pull his blanket across my lap. Instead of a leash, I bring a pen. No pocket full of treats today; instead, I hold hot tea, the blank page, and a decade spilling with memory. In my grief, I will find joy, inhaling, exhaling, smiling thank you, and resolving, one day at a time, to put one foot, ever in front of the other.

TWO

Faithful Heart: Aura

DIANNE HARDY

I'm feline, a smuggled cat, not allowed where I live, Palatial Living. Fancy name for a trailer park, huh? My Mom got me five years ago through a newspaper ad. I came free of charge, didn't cost her one red cent. That made her happy because she's tight, or it might be because she's old—sixty something. Anyway, she rarely talks about money other than to mutter something about it being the root of all evil.

She tries to make me feel guilty when I refuse to eat dry cat food saying, "Don't be ungrateful, Aura. When I was a kid people drowned whole litters of baby cats." I think that's completely off the subject and shouldn't a writer know better? You see, as a baby I was given canned cat food once at my other house and that kind of pleasure stays with you, you know?

∼

Sleeping's my life. Mom claims I do too much, but she's just jealous because she

can't sleep through a night. Needing to pee gets her up and Facebook keeps her up. At three in the morning for Heaven's sake!

She buys stupid toys to intrigue me, like I've forgotten how to play or something. One worked for a short time. A red dot circling the room had me running helter-skelter; until I realized she was controlling the event. That's when I ignored it and between you and me, that was hard.

I'm not your ordinary run-of-the-mill cat. Mom's not ordinary either. We're both gifted…you know, psychically. She says she checked out cats before me and none of them spoke to her soul.

According to her I was crying inconsolably. The kid who was giving me and my siblings away actually tried to dissuade her from choosing me. Pointing, he said, "That one is the smallest, the least ready to wean. She's the runt of the litter."

Mom paid him no attention, simply went with her intuition as usual. As I settled down, nestling comfortably in the palm of her hand, we bonded. On the way home she proclaimed:

> I need you, tiny girl.
> You smoky ball of fluff
> with eyes of karmic bent

to atone my deficit.
You'll be my Aura.

Life hasn't all been rosy. Cats are supposed to be independent. Although embarrassed to admit it, I'm downright needy at times. It's Mom's fault because she's pre-occupied with her music, spending hours at the piano, oblivious to me.

Getting her attention is easier when she talks on the phone and I bite her foot—not hard, just enough to irritate her. She'll yell, "You naughty girl." I just haven't found anything to work where music is involved.

Wikipedia says that "If you can't beat them join them" means admitting defeat and showing a willingness to work with "them." That's what I decided to do with Mom.

I started listening to the music she plays. Much of it is popular stuff from the 1950's—her day, but some is high-brow and technical like the music of Beethoven. To my surprise, I've found I rather like him.

So when she plays the *Moonlight Sonata,* I come running and sing along. Moonlight does that to me, fence or no fence. *Fur Elise* makes me content enough to fall asleep. Mom doesn't notice whether I'm singing or sleeping because, like I said, at the piano she's in her own world.

That Beethoven must have been one talented guy. He wrote beautiful music when he was deaf—by just hearing it in his head. He sounds rather psychic to me, I think maybe he's one of us.

Besides music, Mom's fanatic about books. They're all over the place, even on our bed. I have to say their attraction escapes me. While okay to lie on, they're not like a box you can climb into and hide. Plus, the content! The stuff she reads can give an ordinary person nightmares—stories by Flannery O'Conner or Stephen King. I've decided all authors are disturbed.

On weekends we get company, Mom's kids—Toni, Rachel, and Glen. They treat me like an interloper, rather than a sister, especially Glen, who makes fun of me. I don't know why; I've never done a thing to him. And the grandkids are the worst, hissing back at me, making faces, pointing, and trying to get at my belly. In defense I once bit one and got shut away in the bedroom. I was punished...not him.

In spite of our trials me and Mom have gotten closer over time. You can tell it by simply looking at me, fat and contented like her, I guess. I used to sleep curled up in a ball, but now I lie stretched out flat, even on my back. She laughs and once said, "You're letting it all hang out, huh Aura?"

As I said, she's psychic like me. She knows when the phone's going to ring and who will be calling. Once she ran to comb her hair and put on lipstick, nearly stepped on me. When I yelled in protest, she said, "Get out of my way, company's coming," and sure enough Ted, our writer friend, showed up a minute later. He always says 'hi' to me before he does her—I love him.

Last summer I had a horrendous encounter with a yellow cat. I sat watching a robin out front when this big guy jumped up on my porch. Viciously, we fought through the screen until Mom, hearing the ruckus, chased the ugly one away. I fled under our bed and stayed for hours. Scheech, I wondered if my tail would ever go back to normal.

Mom often sings to me while we're in our cushy blue chair. It's the place in the house where I have her completely to myself. That's because she and I are the only ones that ever sit in it. Long ago Glen gave the chair a bad rap due to my gray hair pasted here and there.

When he says, "Mom, that chair's loaded with cat hair—you need to vacuum it," she obeys, but his efforts to make me look bad don't work. She and I appreciate the blending of blue and gray because we're sensitive to creative expression —art—which he doesn't understand being Obsessive Compulsive, plus an intolerant redneck.

Anyway, Mom owns hundreds of CDs. My all-time favorite is one of Jim Reeves. We were sitting in our chair listening one day. I was dozing in and out, lulled by the opening strains of *Four Walls*. Jim's caressing voice began: "Out where the bright lights are glowing, you're drawn like a moth to a flame..." I shot up, wide awake. A moth? Where? I'd like to get my paws on that.

Last year a major crisis glued me and Mom fast as a flea on a dog. I've always known when she was leaving—even before she hauled out the suitcase. I'd tried lying on top of it in protest. I'd also hidden, refusing to say good-bye, but neither ever kept her home. She'd only stay away for a short time, a couple of days at the most.

Last September when she left, things felt different. Instead of driving her car she went with Glen, and stayed away. Every few days he'd let himself into our house and call, "Where's my good kitty?" like Mom does. The first time it happened I fell for it and came running—but never again.

Hiding under the bed, I thought, Fool me once, shame on you, fool me twice, shame on me. You know I'm pretty smart; I said that better than that one guy—who was he? Oh yeah, Former President George Bush! He was before my time, but Mom must have liked him because she always imitated him in a funny voice and finished with 'heh, heh.'

At our house while Mom was gone, Glen would set out food and fresh water. Then he'd start shoveling crap out of my litter box. Within seconds he'd be cussing like a preacher. Ah, sweet revenge.

Well, the separation wore on both me and Mom. When she came home three weeks later, I was hoarse from crying and wild with fear, not about to let her touch me. Come to think of it, she didn't even try.

She looked scary and wore a big brace on her knee. Even going from our chair to the bathroom, she used her walker and winced with every step. Worse yet, she stared straight ahead all day, no writing, playing the piano—nothing. When the telephone rang, she didn't answer and Glen had to use his key to get in the house because she wouldn't go to the door.

He'd come in, heat up a can of chicken noodle soup and sit and watch her eat it. That's when I knew for certain something was wrong, because she used to eat all the time, even in the night, and now she didn't want to.

After a week Glen was tired of it, pissed off royally in fact. "All right, Mom, you're going to promise me you won't do anything bad or you have to go live with Rachel so she can watch you. Now which will it be?"

When Mom didn't answer, he yelled, "Either way your cat will be gone because none of us kids can take her. We already have animals and she won't be able to adapt. You're all she's got."

Mom looked over at me, seemed to really notice me for the first time in a long time. I quit licking myself and watched her back. After what felt like an eternity she softly said, "I promise, Glen. I won't do anything bad," and broke down crying.

He softened. "I know it's hard. Losing music must feel like death to you, but the doctors say when the drugs are finally out of your system you might be able to play again. We've got to be patient."

All three kids were at our house the following week.

"Well, Mom, you're looking better than you did when you first had the knee replacement," Toni said. "Sorry, I couldn't stay longer. When I left Roosevelt it was quiet but just when you came out of surgery, I got a call from my boss saying we had three to embalm, so I had to leave Logan. I said good-bye to you but I doubt you remember it because you were still under the anesthetic. That's the life of a mortician—I'm always on call whether it's slow or they're dying like flies."

I like that. Once I found one, a fly on the window sill—killed and ate it, slicker than shit!

"When did you notice Mom wasn't all right?" Toni asked Glen.

"She was doing well but in a lot of pain while still in the hospital, so they gave her more drugs," he said.

"Yeah," Rachel agreed. "Two days later they took her to a rehab center to recover. She was on massive doses of Morphine, Valium, and Loritab, all at the same time. We were in her room visiting when someone turned on the TV. It was LDS conference and Mom blurted out, 'Turn that off. It's a conspiracy.'"

Toni laughed. "I've never once heard her use that word."

"We hadn't either," Glen chuckled.

"I still feel bad for the help," said Rachel. "The lady on

night-shift was sweet and caring, but the more patient she was, the worse Mom treated her—called her Nurse Ratchett in Pink."

"Oh, that's terrible," Toni cried, "Do you think she got it?"

Well, Mom stared straight ahead, but I got it; I'm not called Aura for nothing! I looked over at the video of *One Flew Over the Cuckoo's Nest* sitting on the bookcase shelf. Mom loves Jack Nicholson because they're both rebels.

"The nurse was probably too young to know the movie." Rachel said. "At any rate, the place got its fill of Mom, said they couldn't deal with her mental condition if it continued. They told us to start looking into lockdown places, didn't they, Glen?"

"Yep. After a couple of days, the doctor reduced her medication, still she was 'out of it' for awhile. The worst was day four when she met her physical therapist. An attendant told her to wait in a large room where there were no chairs. I think he thought she'd use a wheel chair. But Mom went with a walker and finding no chairs, she sat down on the piano bench.

The therapist came in, introduced himself and seeing her at the piano said,

"Do you play?"

"Yes, she said, smiling and placing her hands on the keys. Glen paused. "Evidently, she couldn't play a note, and she's been suicidal at different times since. The doctor advised us not to push the music playing. He said Mom would know when the time was right to try. It hasn't happened yet."

So that's it! Here I was thinking the problem was her knee. I should have known it was caused by music and that's why I'd catch her staring at the piano. It also explains the day she hugged me hard enough I had trouble breathing. She cried, "Aura, Aura, help me. Music's been with me longer than anything in my life." All I could do was lick her, so I did that until my tongue was sore.

I guess I should be grateful to her kids for finally giving me answers. Nobody tells a cat anything. Over time Mom began to walk better and her appetite came back. When I heard her humming *Stayin' Alive,* I knew we'd make it. Still, I watched her closely and lay on her lap purring—whole days sometimes.

Her thirteenth day home, I awoke to find her shuffling through movies. She reached for *The Hours.* Knowing I'd better do something drastic, I leapt onto the chair, flew over to the shelf, and knocked *Awakenings* to the floor. It's about patients in a hospital for the chronically ill and a doctor who brings them out of a catatonic state.

"Dog-gone-it, Aura. Look what you've done," she yelled, shoving me to the floor. But she picked up the box, thought a moment, and put the movie into the machine. There's a scene where the doctor, Robin Williams, races onto the patients' ward in the middle of the night to find everyone chattering about their lives as though it were forty years before. A man sits at the grand piano playing a Jerome Kern song, *All the Things You Are.*

Mom stared wide-eyed at the TV. Her mouth dropped open. She grabbed the remote and paused the movie. Tossing me from her lap, she rose from our chair and hobbled to the piano.

"I can do that," she declared. Then she played *The Way We Were* as though there'd been no hiatus—laughing and crying at the same time. We didn't even finish the movie.

That was a year ago. Now Glen is having his own crisis. Mom has him come to eat lunch every day because he's depressed and gaunt-looking. I heard her demand that he promise the same thing she promised him—not to do anything bad.

I'm actually getting more used to him. Instead of running to hide when he comes, I stay put on our chair. Mom noticed and told me, "That's good, Aura. You need to be in here with us because we're a family. Maybe you can help him like you did me."

Maybe tragedy changes people. Yesterday he petted me.

THREE

My Cat Has No Good Manners

LAVERN SPENCER MCCARTHY

Don't leap on the table.
Stay out of my plate.
You gobbled your dinner.
You think mine is great.
How could you be hungry
with all that you ate?

You jostled their coffee
when neighbors were here.
You dangled your body
from my chandelier,
then nosed through the dumpster,
ate garbage, I fear.

Stop chewing that ivy
or else it will die.
Don't claw at my pillow

where feathers could fly.
I know you're not perfect,
but please, won't you try?

Come, sit here beside me.
I'll give you a pat.
I'll tickle your tummy,
assuring you that
there's room in my heart
for a bad-mannered cat.

FOUR

Trash Can Tyrant

WOODROW WALTERS

Amongst his fellow feral felines, Kumo was an oddball. He wasn't wary of anything. He welcomed new experiences. That's how we met. I had worked for a pest control company for about a year and a half. I came around the back of an old lady's house to see a garbage can lid filled with meow mix. It was the feeding trough for Kumo and his impromptu family. As I came into view, the cats panicked, darting in different directions, disappearing into the woods. All, that is, but one. I walked closer. I expected him to fly away as well, but he simply looked up, uttered a tiny cry, and went back to eviscerating his food. Food was his whole life.

Kumo lived in a garbage can, and his teeth were rotten. I suspect the rot came from eating things long gone foul. Fevered feasts on the fetid. The pain presented to him by the consumption of hard food was met with brutality in kind. He would shake each piece of kibble, imagining its intangible neck snapping and its will to fight back being crushed beneath his mighty paw. He loved being petted. Once he had finished eating, he would follow me around and rub up against my legs. This made spraying chemicals a bit more difficult, but I enjoyed the company. He quickly became the best part of my day.

One day he came around the side of the house to greet me, tiny claws piercing my pant leg in a wordless, "uppies." Naturally, I complied. He stood on my forearm, nuzzling my chest for a few moments before he looked to the sky cross-eyed and slack-jawed. I almost had time to laugh before he sneezed blood all over my chest. His harsh reality had gifted him a respiratory infection that would've been a death sentence if not treated. I called my wife and asked if I could bring him home with me. I expected resistance, but when she saw his face, she melted just like I had. His soul filled a hole in our family we didn't know we had. He spent the rest of the day resting beneath the heater in my van.

Now toothless save for his canines, Kumo stalked the halls of our home at all hours hunting for potential prey. Nothing could sate him. His new favorite foods were Sour Patch Kids, freshly unattended yogurt, and uncooked marinating steaks. He had even taught himself how to get inside a garbage can. We bought one with a lid. It made no difference.

We keep the baking supplies on the shelf fifth from the ground. I have to reach above my head to pull them down. This distance meant nothing to my intrepid interloper. He must have pounced and scrabbled his way up from one shelf to another until he reached them.

When I arrived home, he was waiting for me at the door, as usual. What was unusual was that he couldn't keep his balance. He swayed back and forth, at times having to catch himself from falling over outright.

It took me an hour to find the chocolate chips on the floor of the cupboard. He had eaten half the bag. He had lethally poisoned himself. Neither my wife, nor I had been home since that morning, so I had no context for how long ago he'd eaten them.

No answer for the vet meant no answer for me when I asked, "Will he even last the drive?"

We rushed to the closest emergency vet. An hour-and-twenty-minute drive. Decorum in these types of situations is to say, "If you had waited one more minute, he might not have made it." They didn't have the time. He stayed with them for four days.

Meanwhile, I came home to a clean house and an empty litter box. No tiny roars of welcome, no scratching on the door frames, and no rubbing against my legs.

Tending to him required keeping his tiny body's heat and heart rate at levels where his organs could function. A constant effort, from what I've been told.

When he finally came home, he had two shaved spots: one on each arm. The fur never grew back, but his love for danger did the next day. He was back in the garbage can in no time.

We assumed his brush with death might have changed something in him. We were wrong. Kumo had no need to learn lessons. The world was wrong, not him. Five days after he got home, I returned from work to find the baking supplies scattered all over the kitchen. The little tyrant had returned to the same basket which had nearly killed him. We had moved the chocolate chips into the cupboard, but we hadn't thought to move the baking supplies. Luckily, arrowroot powder and flour didn't appeal to him like the chocolate chips had. He wasn't ashamed of the mess. He just rushed to the door to greet me, as always. His little claws cut into my leg and all I could say was,

"You're going to be the death of me, buddy."

FIVE

Horse Girl

E.B. WHEELER

Growing up, I was a bit of a tomboy, playing cul-de-sac baseball with the neighborhood boys and scrambling around the woods and creeks in northern Georgia, but in at least one way, I was a typical girl: I wanted a pony.

Or, really, a horse.

I begged to spend each birthday party and summer camp at the local riding stable. I read every horse book I could find —fiction or non-fiction—until I was a walking encyclopedia of horse facts. To my mother's sorrow, I wasn't interested in dolls unless they could sit on my toy horses—which evolved from colorful My Little Ponies to realistic and collectible Breyer models.

The enjoyment of guiding rented horses through tree-lined trails or currying their coats to a show-worthy gloss wasn't enough. My dreams of horse ownership shone with the promise of freedom. Climbing into the saddle and riding off whenever and wherever I wanted in harmony with my loyal and intelligent companion. I had a favorite horse at the riding stable, but it would be something truly special if the horse were mine. Like in the Linda Craig Adventures—one of my favorite horse book series—I dreamed of rescuing hapless tourists, solving mysteries, and discovering lost treasures, all with the aid of my trusty equine partner.

When we moved from the lush, green woods of Georgia to the brown desert of Southern California in my tween years, I found only one consolation: our new home stood on almost an acre. Horse property.

Some kids in my new neighborhood even had horses, providing new chances to ride. But these were still borrowed mounts. I measured and sketched out plans, showing my parents how easily we could fit a stall and corral in our large yard. But all my powers of persuasion weren't enough to convince them. Our horse property remained horseless.

They did agree that I could take riding lessons again, but finding a stable in California proved more difficult—apparently, fear of lawsuits stifled horse rentals. If I wanted lessons, I needed a horse of my own.

Finally, one of the stables I called offered an odd kind of salvation.

"Do you have a horse?" the manager asked.

"No," I admitted. "But I'd really like to take lessons."

She was quiet for a minute. She was a horse girl, too, after all. She knew the longing. "I have an idea that might help both of us."

This stable had a horse that didn't belong to anyone. His

name was Anazor—Zor for short—a light grey half-Arabian with the elegant head and energetic gait of his breed. His former owners had divorced. Neither wanted the horse, so they abandoned him at the boarding stable. The stable owner couldn't sell him because she didn't have proof of ownership, especially not with his upper lip tattooed for identification.

She was stuck with a horse she had to board for free, and I was looking for a horse to take lessons with. She couldn't sell him to me, and I couldn't afford the cost of boarding a horse in addition to lessons, but we struck a deal. I worked at the stable on Saturdays, mucking out stalls, grooming and exercising horses, and cleaning the clubhouse, and Zor would be "my" horse—I would take care of him, and I could use him for lessons and riding. Good enough for me!

So began my magical partnership. Zor was only a little better than green-broke, but that's where the lessons came in. We were learning together. I sometimes took him on trail rides through the desert dunes with other students at the stables. It turns out those lip tattoos are primarily meant to identify potential racehorses. Zor wanted to *go*, and I loved it. We left the quarter horses in the desert dust on those sandy trails.

But my horse girl fantasies called for something more. More adventure.

Be careful what you wish for, as they say.

My opportunity came in the form of a local Fourth of July parade. A group of people in my neighborhood would be riding their horses in the parade, and I decided to join them.

The parade route was nine or ten miles from the stable, with the bed of the Mojave River a convenient connector bypassing the busy streets. I would have my adventure riding Zor up to the parade, then return him to the stables.

I estimated how long the ride would take and arrived in the early morning stillness to brush Zor to a shine and weave red, white, and blue ribbons in his pale grey mane and tail. Once I had him looking splendid enough even for the Tournament of Roses parade, we set off in the cool morning air of the high desert.

The Mojave River looks dry most of the year, but it flows underground. The open, sandy corridor of the river appears flat and inviting, yet it's soft in places, almost like quicksand—dangerous for a horse who might sink or trip and break its leg. I had to keep Zor toward the bank where the ground was firm. Yet along the bank, we had to navigate low-hanging cottonwood branches and the occasional marshy bits, which stink like rotting cottonwood leaves and algae. I needed Zor to trust me enough to guide him around these obstacles.

He did not.

He saw all that open space, and he wanted to run. It was a constant battle to turn him back for the safe sand along the edges of the riverbed. Sometimes we turned in circles. And then, trying to convince him not to splash through the occasional mucky spot? It was beginning to get hot—the desert warms up fast in July—so they must have looked inviting, but I couldn't tell how deep they went, and that was some nasty water to splash in or drink. Zor's lovely ribbons drooped, and his coat had definitely lost its glossy shine. We both dripped with sweat. I'm pretty sure he was trying to scrape me off on the cottonwoods when we came across them. I was learning why people who work with horses use colorful language. Part of me wanted to let him knock me off and just watch the stupid creature run off and break his legs…

No, no, no. I didn't really want that. I just wanted him to listen to me. I wanted us to be the kind of partners that dreams—my horse-girl dreams—were made of. In The Saddle Club books and the Linda Craig Adventures, girl and horse worked together through difficult terrain and survived against the odds. The rider could give the horse its head, and it would lead them to safety.

Zor would lead me into a stinky quagmire.

Dreams melt fast when the sun's glare is in your eyes and sweat rolls between your shoulder blades. We struggled on, slowly, fighting each other the whole way. By the time I reached my house, the parade was long over. I'm not sure if I should be impressed or concerned that my parents hadn't come looking for me.

I slid off Zor's back, my legs trembling, throat parched, and muscles aching in new and interesting places, even for someone used to riding. My family was there, my younger brothers vaguely curious about the animal, and my dad experienced enough with horses to help me get Zor watered and cooled off.

Finally, the day wore on, and my relief at being home knitted itself into a growing anxiety. I had to get Zor back to the stables.

"Do you want me to take him?" my dad asked, interested in a shot at riding a lively but stubborn horse.

I knew I should return Zor myself. Weren't we partners, teammates, destined to be best friends? No. Exhausted, heat sick, and a little heartsick, I admitted to myself that I didn't have the physical or emotional stamina to manage the ride back.

"Thank you," I told my dad and watched as he rode Zor off.

Maybe Zor was too tired to misbehave, maybe he was just as awful then as he had been for me, maybe my dad was the better rider. If my dad mentioned what the return journey was like, I don't recall.

My only pictures of Zor came from that day, someone in the family snapping a few shots of Zor at our house. I continued working at the stable and taking care of Zor through that summer, but high school was fast approaching. Friends, music, boys, and other new interests took me away from the stables more and more. Part of me was sorry, and I missed Zor a little, but I resented him a little, too. Because what I really missed was the dream that Zor had represented, and it dimmed in the light of day as most dreams do.

But flashes of it resurface all these years later. I sold most of my Breyer horses to help pay for a post-high school trip to England, but I still keep a few favorites on my shelf. I've taken my own girls to ride on docile stable horses, though they're not passionate about the sport. It's probably for the best. My husband is allergic to horses, and I now have a spinal injury that bars me from rollercoasters, skydiving, and horseback riding. Yet sometimes I stop to watch a horse grazing or trotting through a pasture, and I daydream. As if I could brush out that shaggy winter coat, feel the tickle of its lips on my palm as it accepted my offered bribe of a carrot or apple, and swing up to ride bareback into some waiting adventure.

SIX

Homing Instinct

SHAROLYN RICHARDS

I moved away from home several times in my life and found it odd when my definition of home changed. When I was young, my home was my parents' house. When I was in college, it was my apartment. Now home is with my husband and my kids, no matter where we live. Home is where we feel secure and safe and perhaps even loved. The phenomenon of home was illustrated to me by a surprising source: pigeons.

I never thought about pigeons. Never thought my husband, Tyler, would want pigeons, but when he got his new puppy, Scout, he was determined to do right by this dog by training it well. He said he needed pigeons for the dog to practice tracking and pointing. I didn't know why he couldn't just use the birds on the mountain. Scout seemed equipped to find those well enough.

A short time later, I found a stack of miniature framed walls. Was Tyler making a playhouse for our kids?

I kicked at the wood. "What's this?"

"My pigeon coop," Tyler replied.

"Your what?" I asked, sure I had misheard. Maybe he had said chicken coop, but we hadn't discussed getting chickens.

"My pigeon coop," he repeated. "I told you I wanted to get pigeons."

Yes, he had mentioned pigeons to help train the dog, but I hadn't thought he was so serious that he would have walls ready to put up a coop within the week.

"When are you getting pigeons? How much are they?"

I couldn't wrap my brain around the idea of having pigeons. I grew up with chickens. Chickens were useful. They gave you eggs. Then if you got tired of them, you could eat them.

I wondered what pigeons would taste like. Would Tyler make me eat them? Could we eat their eggs? How often did they lay eggs? If it was every day and we had baby pigeons, what would we do with them all? I stepped back as the weight of all these questions hit me. Did he know what he was getting himself into?

"Five to ten dollars a bird, depending on where I get them."

"Okay," I said slowly.

"My dad will help take care of them. We need them to train the dogs."

I turned away before I rolled my eyes. I never would understand the hunter's mind.

Before I knew it, Tyler announced he would get pigeons with the kids while I was at a conference. Of course, the kids were excited, and by the time I got home, they had them all named. All the pigeons looked different, but I wasn't sure I would ever remember the names of ten birds.

During the first two weeks, I almost forgot we had pigeons, except for the coop standing next to the barn, which I could easily see out my kitchen window.

"Today is the test," Tyler announced. "I'll let them out, and we'll see if they return."

"I hope they come back. If they don't, you wasted your money."

"They should come back." Tyler tried to sound confident, but I could tell he was a little nervous. There was a part of him that wondered if they really would return. I didn't care if they came back, but I also didn't want to see Tyler disappointed over a failed pigeon experiment.

Apparently, they didn't go far. The following Saturday, Tyler came in from working in the garage. "A cat got one of the pigeons. The stupid birds just sit on the ground instead of on the barn or fence."

The following Saturday, I saw him run out to the pasture with his long strides. I stopped washing dishes and let the water run, mesmerized by his strange actions. He leaped on the flatbed trailer parked next to the pigeon coop. He jumped up and down on the trailer, making it shake, his mouth moving. He looked like a toddler throwing a fit. A blur streaked out from under the trailer and disappeared before I could identify it.

I slipped on my shoes and met him at the garage door.

"I need to trap a cat," he said, his face slightly red.

"Did another cat get a pigeon?" I asked, the puzzle pieces coming together.

"It was the same cat. I saw him coming, so I ran out to the pasture. The cat got the pigeon and dragged it under the trailer. After I jumped on the trailer and yelled, the cat ran away, and I was able to get the pigeon. Just his wing is injured; maybe it'll be okay."

That explained his strange actions, and I giggled a little, releasing my tension. The pigeon might survive. I didn't want Tyler to lose a pigeon so soon.

"I'm going to trap that cat and find it a new place to live," Tyler said.

That made sense to me. We didn't buy the pigeons for cat food. Would I see a message on Facebook looking for a lost cat? I couldn't think about that. We had dumb pigeons who sat on the ground instead of roosting on the barn roof to save.

"I checked the trap," Tyler said as he sat next to me at one of our kids' flag football games a couple of days later. "I caught the cat. I found a new home for it about twenty miles away."

"What if it comes back?" I asked.

"Cats aren't that smart," he said.

Was it just me, or was it ironic that we expected the no-so-smart cat not to make its way back home when our dumb pigeons were supposed to do precisely that?

I fought thinking the pigeons were pets. I didn't want to get too attached. Then the hawk came. Tyler and I watched it flutter against the coop windows, wondering if it would get in. Why we didn't go out immediately to scare it away, I don't know, but we watched in a sort of horrified fascination until the hawk found its way into the one-way door that let the pigeons in and not out.

"Go! Go!" I yelled, too shocked to think of any other word.

Tyler ran out, barefoot, to the coop and opened the door.

"Get out of here!" he yelled.

Pigeons flew past him, followed by what I assumed was a very bewildered hawk.

I stood in the open door to our house and watched him come back.

"Were the babies okay?" I asked, remembering he had told me we had two baby pigeons in a nest.

"I'm not sure, I didn't want to go in barefoot."

I had my shoes on. Don't ask why I wasn't the one to run out. Scared of being dive-bombed by a hawk probably. I slowly opened the pigeon door. There was one older pigeon still in the coop, alive. At least one stayed to protect the babies. I looked in the nest and watched the babies to make sure they were breathing. Relief flowed through me as the rise and fall of their little bodies told me they were safe.

Now, each morning as the pigeons are released from the coop I find it relaxing to watch them swoop out of the coop, fly over the house, and circle back to the barn to land on the roof. They move together in one fluid movement.

Every night, the pigeons return to their home. No matter how far they fly, they know how to come home again.

They know where home is. They know where they would be safe and fed.

I sometimes drive home to find them lined up on the roof of our house as if they are welcoming me. Those are the times I feel an intense feeling of belonging. The pigeons have become the symbol of all the feelings associated with home.

    I never expected to learn such a profound lesson from pigeons, but they know where their home is. Even as I have moved around, I have always felt the need to identify some place as home. Just as pigeons can adjust to a new place and consider that their home base, I did the same as I moved from my parent's house to college and then when I got married and made my own home.

SEVEN

Live Streaming

JOHN SAVOIE

The final time we walked
the Gardens, stiff-hipped,
nearly deaf, mostly blind,
you turned toward the sun,
nostrils twitched and flared,
eyes squinched, and the wind
lifted your broad black ears
as if wings spread for flight,
the grey fringes tasseling
in streams of golden light.

EIGHT

A Tale of Tails: How I (Almost) Overcame My Canine Phobia

EDMOND PORTER

I sat on the sofa in the single-wide mobile home, a colossal Rottweiler only inches from my face, staring at me. A string of saliva hung from the corner of his mouth, swaying like a pendulum. He swung his head from side to side as if he were drooling over a piece of fresh meat. A wave of panic washed over me, and I shifted on the sofa, trying to avoid any eye contact that might upset the animal.

Our church leaders assigned me and my neighbor to visit this family monthly. I scheduled the visit but wasn't prepared to face a massive dog in a confined space. While my neighbor and the family's father engaged in friendly conversation, sweat trickled down my back, and my breaths grew shallow and fast; I barely heard the discussion in the room. All I could focus on was managing my fear of dogs and urging the time to pass.

How did I, a normally functioning adult in most circumstances, get into such a predicament? To answer that,

I need to go back to my childhood or, more like, my toddlerhood. The inciting incident doesn't even register in my memory, so I will rely on the story I was told.

My aunt had a little dog. Cindy—the dog, not my aunt—had short black hair. Her pedigree was unknown, but she was a faithful companion and followed my aunt everywhere. Well, not to school, I guess, but I was never at school with her, so that doesn't count. We were at the ranch while Daddy and Grandpa were milking the cows, and I, a two-year-old, was playing with the dog outside the barn. I twisted her tail, and she growled and snapped at me, but I thought she was playing. So, I continued the game. But Cindy had other ideas. With lightning speed, her teeth sunk into my chin. I shrieked, bringing Daddy rushing from the barn and sweeping me into his arms.

Dogs frightened me from then on, but a strange thing happened. A few years later, Uncle George, Daddy's uncle, visited us at the ranch. He stopped his team of horses in front of the barn and pulled a cardboard box from the wagon. He said he had a surprise for me. He set the box down and opened the flaps. Inside were five of the cutest little puppies I'd ever seen. One was furry and white with tan markings around its face and ears. It looked at me with curious brown eyes that drew me in. I wanted to touch it, but I was afraid. What if it bit me? What if it growled or barked at me? I moved closer, then farther away, then closer again, unsure of what to do.

Daddy saw my hesitation and knelt beside me.

He gently pushed me toward the box and whispered, "If you pick up a puppy, you can have it."

My hand went out and then pulled back. I tried again. This time, I felt the softness of the fur, and then I felt something else, something warm and wet. The puppy licked my hand, and I jerked it away. I took a deep breath and mustered all the courage a five-year-old boy could summon. I trembled as I reached out again, my hand wrapping around the warm, squirming body. Then it was in my hands, and I lifted it from the box. It wriggled in my arms, but it didn't bite me. It didn't bark. And then it snuggled against me and made a soft, contented sound. I hugged it closely and held it all the way home.

Powder Puff, named for his softness and markings, was my friend. Over the next few weeks, he grew from a little fur ball into a bouncing puppy. We played together for hours, chasing each other around the yard and rolling in the grass. But one day, he was gone. I searched everywhere for him, but I couldn't find him. I called his name, but he didn't come. I felt a knot in my stomach and a lump in my throat.

Mother joined in the search, but after we covered the yard the third time, she hitched my little sister higher on her hip and wrapped her other arm around me. "Don't worry; Daddy will help you find Powder Puff when he gets home from work."

"Are you sure?" I asked, fighting back tears.

"Yes," Mother said, giving me another squeeze.

I sat on the front porch, waiting and hoping. I wrapped my arms around my knees, wondering where Powder Puff was. Finally, Daddy's green Mercury pulled into the driveway. I jumped up and ran to him.

My words spilled out along with the tears. "Powder Puff

is missing. I've looked for him all over the yard and can't find him anywhere."

Daddy looked at me with a serious expression. "Go inside. I'll look for him." He lifted my chin and gazed into my eyes. "I'll be back soon." His voice was calm, but I could hear the worry in it.

I nodded and ran into the house.

When Daddy returned, his face was grim. He held Powder Puff in his arms, but my puppy didn't move. He didn't breathe. He was gone. Daddy told me what had happened, how a car had hit him. I felt a wave of grief wash over me, and I threw myself on the sofa. I buried my face into the cushions and sobbed. Mother and Daddy tried to comfort me, but I couldn't stop the tears.

Later, Daddy helped me carry the puppy to the hole he'd dug in the backyard. We laid him gently on the ground and covered him with dirt. We placed a rock on the grave and solemnly returned to the house.

As time passed, the pain eased, and I decided I was through with dogs. But they weren't through with me.

Sometime after losing Powder Puff, my older brother and I were playing with our friends the Knapps at their house. They had a big, hairy dog that constantly barked and chased after me, unlike my puppy. I tried to be brave in front of my friends and brother, but I was terrified. We played games in the backyard until I felt a sharp pain. I grabbed my butt and screamed in terror. The dog had bitten me.

Mrs. Knapp bolted out of the house, the door banging behind her.

"What happened?" she demanded.

"The dog bit him," my friend said, pointing at me.

"I need to check the injury," Mrs. Knapp said, dragging me through the door and into the kitchen. "Pull down your pants."

I hesitated, but her stare forced me to unfasten my belt and tug down my jeans. I felt naked even though I was still wearing my briefs, the humiliation almost worse than the bite.

She studied the wound. "It doesn't look too bad," she said, clicking her tongue. "It didn't even break the skin."

Her words did little to comfort me, but she smeared some ointment on my buttocks and sent me back out to play, the dog now chained to a tree.

The bite didn't leave a scar, but the memory did, and my fear turned into a phobia. I had been bitten on both ends of my body and dreaded the thought of experiencing something like that again. From then on, I avoided dogs as much as possible, crossing the street when I saw one or declining invitations to visit friends who owned dogs. I became a master at avoidance techniques.

Years passed, and I had children who begged for a dog. However, my fear of dogs had not dissipated because I was a dad. I wanted to give my children a normal childhood, so I agreed to let them have a couple of dogs at different times, but neither worked out.

The first was Daisy, a tan, short-haired mutt we rescued from the pound. She was friendly and gentle, and the kids adored her, but one day, another dog attacked her while we were walking her in the neighborhood. The sight and sounds of the attack triggered all the anxiety I'd ever felt around dogs.

The second was Bo, a neurotic Cocker Spaniel with curly fur and big brown eyes. He also had severe allergies that made him scratch and sneeze all the time. He needed medicine, special food, and grooming, which cost a fortune. We eventually re-homed him to a loving family with more patience and dog experience.

I congratulated myself for surviving each encounter with the Rottweiler on our monthly visits. But, after a few months, I was elated when I was reassigned to visit a different family who did not own a dog.

While I endured these dogs, I was relieved when I was dog-free again.

However, three of my five children grew up to be dog lovers and owners. Whenever we visited them, I tried to make the best of it and accept their dogs, but the real challenge came last summer. My youngest daughter and her husband went to Hawaii on vacation and asked us to dog-sit their two dogs for ten days.

They were smaller mixed-breed dogs with long fur, one black and the other a deep chocolate brown. Their fur smelled of damp earth and kibble, and they barked at every sound and movement. I was not thrilled about the arrangement, but I agreed for my daughter's sake. I knew she would feel better if we cared for them rather than sending them to a boarding kennel. However, I was unprepared for the first night when the dogs jumped on the bed and settled in. They snored like chainsaws, drooled on the quilt, and occupied most of the space. I surprised my wife by letting them stay on the bed, even though I was uncomfortable and annoyed.

After a few days of sharing our home with the dogs, a subtle change began to unfold. Initially unfamiliar and awkward, their presence gradually became part of the daily routine, and I looked forward to their greeting at the door, their tails wagging in eager salutation.

Around the house, they became my silent companions, shadowing my every move. When I settled onto the couch, they'd leap up, their paws searching for purchase, and nuzzle into the cozy nooks. Their eyes, wide and imploring, begged for belly rubs. I succumbed to their pleading eyes and indulged them.

Outside, they became little adventurers, tugging at their leashes as soon as they were clipped on. They'd bound forward with contagious enthusiasm, exploring patches of grass, fire hydrants, and cracks in the sidewalk, their ears perked and their tails beating time like a metronome. And I'd watch, marveling at their simple delight in the world around them.

Yes, they sometimes acted like spoiled children, their heads tilted, demanding treats. And if I hesitated, they'd give me those patented puppy-dog eyes, liquid pools of longing that melted my resolve.

As the ten days came to an end, I discovered that these dogs had transformed into more than mere pets. They had become distinct individuals, each with their own personality and emotions. And when the day came for them to return to their own home, an unexpected loss settled in. The house suddenly felt quieter, emptier. These furry companions had truly grown on me.

Now, please don't misunderstand me. Dog sitting for ten days didn't erase my deep-rooted fear of dogs built up over a lifetime, but it and other positive interactions have helped me cope with my phobia and accept dogs as part of my life. Still, I can't help but wonder: if faced with a Rottweiler's imposing gaze in a single-wide mobile home today, would I handle it differently than I did twenty-five years ago? I don't know, and I sincerely hope I never have to find out.

NINE

Lady Meow

MICHAEL OBORN

Maybe she wasn't a people proper, but she exhibited the qualities and characteristics of a people.

A pall of sadness hangs heavy over this house this day. As the sun rose, the cat's lights dimmed. She had fallen off the bed and could no longer stand. Knowing something was very wrong, she was trembling.

Gina wrapped her in a towel and tried to make her comfortable until morning when she could take her to the vet. The last thing we wanted was that she suffer.

Gina is a cat magnet. She makes a special noise cats can't seem to resist. When we walk in the neighborhood, we are required to make several petting stops as we go. She pets each cat, and we meander on to the next. If a cat follows, she indulges it with another caressing. Not much of a walk as I stand around while the neighborhood cats get all her attention. Jealousy extant.

It had been months since our old gray and white cat

failed to come home. It, too, was another of my sweetheart's rescue missions.

One afternoon, Gina met me at the door. "We have a new boarder." Pause. "I couldn't help it."

One of Gina's quilting friends had passed. When the family of that friend found her, three days had lapsed. No visitors during those three days. The cat had been with her the whole time.

The cat was an older, classic Egyptian, dark with flecks of yellow, gold, and orange.

She cautiously acclimated to us. I gave her a respectable space while Gina petted the hell out of her.

The first few days, she sat, a stoic sphinx, on the exact middle stair between upstairs where Gina spends most of her days working on some fabric creation (she teaches sewing), and down where my office is.

While she tolerated me, a bond grew between them.

Never having been a cat person, I have been forced to amend my position on the feline species.

The cat learned our daily routine and would monitor our activities and whereabouts at regular intervals. Finally comfortable with us, she sleeps two hours, then comes to check on me where I write. Does the same with my honey. She will come, sit, and stare at me as if I were an art piece. I ask her if everything is cool. She says nothing. I call her Lady Meow.

After a time, she began to talk to me in the A.M. I'm told Egyptians do that. One chatty morning, I put a few treats down. She didn't touch them but instead sat staring directly at me. After a while, it became a little disconcerting. I called upstairs, asked Gina if everything was okay. She confirmed it was. Nothing left to do but approach the problem head-on.

"Alright Lady, what's going on? Be a little more specific, please. I'm busy here."

Lady Meow, having no doubt had it with stupidity, lifted her chin half an inch and pranced out of my office. I wondered what I said that had offended. It had been three hours.

Lady Meow was the only cat I've known that did not tolerate our presence because we fed her. She was more like an alien from some distant planet placed here to study our species. There was something all-knowing that commanded respect, a silent dignity I could not deny.

Until last week she would talk to us, monitor our whereabouts, and command us to pet her at certain intervals during the evening when I imagine she felt *we* needed it. She would slink cautiously like an eel between Gina and I on the couch, pause for a moment, then put one paw on Gina's leg and wait. Truly, I am not making this up. Gina would set her sewing down, gently bring her to her lap, and commence a five-minute caressing session. I won't say I was jealous, but I should be so lucky.

For the past two months, Lady Meow's sight had been failing. She would wait until I moved before approaching me. Allowing us to pet her was our blessing. This last week it was as though she knew. She stopped eating. Gina would give her tuna water.

As we pass each other this morning we stop and hug. Gina is carrying a hanky that looks to need wringing out.

Never did tell you what Lady Meow did the second night

in her new home with us. Must have been three A.M. I felt a slight motion of the bed. I opened an eye. Lady Meow was looking at me. I didn't move. She went to Gina and placed her whiskers next to her nose. After a few moments, she did the same with me.

Believe this—she slept on Gina's chest as if the rhythm of her breathing was some kind of comfort.

I still shudder thinking about those last three days she lived with her last owner.

Can't help but respect what she'd been through. What a giant honor it was to have known her.

A pall of sadness hangs over this house this day.

TEN

Geronimo!

SHERRIE GAVIN

"It will be like you don't even have a dog," promised my husband.

Bruce was desperate for a dog. I even wondered if that is why he pressed for us to sell our Sydney apartment for a house that was four train stops further away from the city, work, and friends. Our new house kissed the edge of Heathcote National Park and greeted us with sightings of Yellow-Tail Black Cockatoos, the occasional kangaroo or wallaby, and the even rarer wombat. It also had many spaces to walk and play with dogs, and we did not need a building association's permission to have a pet.

I was hesitant. "I just don't want to do all the extra cleaning..."

"You won't," he interrupted.

"And I'm working on the PhD..."

"I know." He guaranteed, "I support you."

Gah. The guilt trip. He was supporting me, so I felt like I needed to support him. I did not like feeling as though I were parenting my husband, making him ask for permission. We were newlyweds, only married for about three years, and I felt like we were still learning the best ways to communicate and support each other. I moved to Australia after I met the handsome bloke and had not found the transition from my home in the United States to be easy. Many Australians simply did not like Americans, so I learned to be very careful when speaking, lest someone hear my accent and begin a diatribe on all that they thought was wrong with whomever the current American president was. It was exhausting. After a year of rejected job applications ("no Australian experience") and working odd jobs, I finally landed a position where I taught one class per term at a local community college. I was trying to keep busy, but I was lonely.

Loneliness was probably the real reason for my hesitation. A dog seemed to signal permanency, and I secretly longed to move home to soda fountains of bottomless frothing root beer, the delicacy of American peanut butter slathered inside celery ribs, and the deliciousness of cheap bread sticks bought by the bag to be dipped in pizza sauce and shared with friends over a long night's mixed conversation about all things utterly silly and completely important. A dog felt permanent. Isolating. Maybe even... responsible? Was I really grown up enough for this next step?

I chuckled at myself. As a life-long diabetic (diagnosed

just before my second birthday), I had always been complimented for my mature sense of responsibility. So I wondered why, after already a lifetime of diabetes, an international move, marriage, a mortgage, and hoped-for parenthood, I felt like this was…too much responsibility. I could find no reason.

"Okay," I said, and within seconds, Bruce was showing me all of the research he had done.

Within a few days, we had an appointment to go and "meet" a litter of four-week-old puppies. The breeder had a great reputation; she lived in a village called Taralga, which was on the Southern Tableland of New South Wales, meaning it was two hours' drive away. The breeder had supplied English Labrador puppies for Assistance Dogs International, and because she lived far from the suburbs of Sydney, her pups were modestly priced compared to city breeders. The Assistance Dogs thing was what appealed most to Bruce.

"It means these dogs will be really good family dogs," he assured me as I eyed the price per puppy. "Good personally and very trainable."

By the next day, Bruce had arranged a meet and greet to see the puppies and make a final choice. We left late-morning on a Saturday and planned to be home well before dinnertime.

For the neophyte: Six-week-old puppies are probably the most hypnotizing creatures in existence. I wanted to be disinterested, tolerant, maybe even cool. But as a lowly mortal, the tiny baby barks, cartoon-like romping, and captivating curiosity of the pups made me instantaneously forget every problem that ever happened in my life—or the entire history of the world—for at least the thirty minutes we were there.

Within what seemed like seconds, but was probably at least thirty minutes (I swear—super powers—puppies stop time!), Bruce arranged to purchase one of the downy blonde boys, reassuring me, "I'll walk him and clean up after him, and he'll be my dog. Dogs choose who in the family is the person, so it will be me because..."

He went on to explain his innate canine kinship before resharing happy stories about his childhood dogs and his natural powers of pooch connection. By the time we were home again, the puppy endorphins had worn off, and I was quite content for Bruce to arrange for and set up the things he knew a dog would need: mat, bowl, crate, towels, blanket, brush, and other things that I quickly lost interest in.

Over the next two weeks, we had updates from the breeder about how the puppies were progressing and the necessary vaccinations they were being given (of which she would provide records for us).

Meanwhile, Bruce and I debated dog names. We searched Australian Aboriginal names and terms, but none felt right. One evening, remembering the puppies jumping and hopping and they tumbled together, Bruce said, "Geronimo." Brave, resilient, protector of families were the descriptors on a baby naming webpage.

"We will finally have our family," he said, noting our shared pain at our inability to conceive. "And American," he added with a wink.

I smiled more than I had in months, and the name was decided.

Our bouncing baby barker turned shy when we placed him in the car. He wept a bit as we drove him away from his biological siblings and birth mama. His whimpers pricked my ears and heart, so I decided to sit in the back seat with him as Bruce drove. I didn't mind; even though I had been in Australia for three years, driving on the left still felt foreign, and empty back lanes sometimes made me forget which side of the street I should be on. Plus, Bruce liked to drive. I had not ever bonded with a dog before, so... can't hurt to try, right? I soothed and cooed as we drove, making Bruce jealous enough that he decided to stop along a grassy patch of traffic-free, old highway that was closer to dirt than the shadow of pavement that had been installed in a past life. We sat on the soft, country green for a few minutes while our fluffy adoptee sniffed everything, looking worried.

"It's okay," Bruce soothed. "We love you."

And we did.

Bruce worked on-site at a commercial bakery, in distribution. Though he primarily worked with trucks and truck drivers, it was still a food production plant, so animals were not allowed. I, on the other hand, was allowed to bring my pup with me when I taught my single class at the college, and because I did not have enough status for an office and was outlining my possible dissertation, I primarily worked from home.

Bruce and I giggled about how I would tell Geronimo to sit, and he would, but Geronimo would not sit for Bruce. I was enjoying looking after the pup, but within two weeks, I was wearing thin on house training. We followed the Assistance Dog Training Guide, and for the most part, things were going well, with only the odd accident. I preferred this method of training because it forbade yelling at or striking the dog in any way, but I was growing frustrated with being awakened to the sound of lonely puppy whimpers.

We set the dog crate up in our bedroom, next to our ensuite. I liked sleeping on the side of the bed closest to the bathroom, so Geronimo was closest to me. Bruce always seemed to sleep through the puppy cries, but I could not. I ended up grabbing a pillow and spare blanket, then falling asleep beside the meshed door of the crate, with Geronimo pressed against the webbing so that his fur poked out and tickled my nose. Only then would the furbaby settle, sleeping beside me, only a thin net of wire between us. It was not a comfortable way for me to sleep, and I was becoming irritable and achy after these nights. In my tired and tender state, I began to regret agreeing to adopt a dog.

Bruce was always surprised to find I had slept on the floor—again. "I didn't hear anything," he would say, scratching his head and yawning.

I did not find this to be particularly romantic. But, in another few weeks, I was finally able to sleep in my bed again. It felt liberating! I felt like I had a month of sleep to catch up on, so one night after a long day, I fell very quickly into a deep sleep. And then. The whimpering.

"Oh, come on!" I said aloud.

Bruce, like usual, was purring in a light snore, refusing to be roused.

"Ssshhhhhh!" I chided.

But the whimpering increased. I was in no mood to sleep on the floor, so I rolled over, commanding, "Quiet!"

But Geronimo's whimpers were becoming incessant.

Assistance Dog Training Guide instructed that any nighttime whimpers past the "settling in" stage should be dealt with by taking the puppy outside for a "toilet run." No eye contact, only give the command to "toilet," then back to bed after the pup had pooped or wee'd, or three minutes, whichever came first. I had done this for a few nights after Geronimo first allowed me to sleep in my bed, but on this night, I had taken him out for a "toilet run" just before bed. Yet the audible puppy pestering was there. I waited for Bruce, even nudging him, but he was completely out of it.

"Okay, okay," I grumbled, rolling out of bed.

I was very unhappy. This was the last straw. I was so tired that I was angry. I let the pup out of his prison and led him through the house, flipping on an outside light. The brightness annoyed me even further, and I stood on the grass and commanded, "TOILET."

Geronimo sat.

"Toilet," I said again, less angry, wondering if my tone had confused him. Still nothing. "Toilet. Toilet...."

The drizzle of patience remaining in me was draining as my feet became more and more chilled by the damp night grass. But the growing wetness of my toes awakened me just a little...enough to notice that Geronimo looked worried. He whimpered again.

"Okay," I said, giving up. "No toilet."

I turned to walk inside and felt his fur shadowing my

heels. As I reached to turn off the outside light, I glanced at my diabetic blood sugar monitor.

"Might as well test," I grumbled to Geronimo.

I closed the sliding back door and stepped into the kitchen, making my way to the stove light. I had used the stove light like this for years—the light was bright enough to see my monitor and even take a shot without any issue, but not bright enough to disrupt a sleeping house or blind my drowsy eyes. As I grabbed the lancer to poke a tiny drop from my least fortunate finger of the moment, I saw Geronimo looking keenly at me. He was not sitting but at full alert.

"You're supposed to be asleep," I told him, as I slid a tiny test strip into the device.

Within 30 seconds, my monitor beeped. My blood sugar was low. Very low. Dangerously low...deathly low. I opened the fridge and grabbed a bottle of apple juice. Removing the lid, I slid to the floor and began to guzzle.

My parents always taught me to get on the floor as quickly as possible when my blood sugar was low. If no one was around, I was supposed to crawl and cry out for help. Being on the floor lessened my chances of earning a broken bone or another injury if I fell as a result of collapsing or passing out before help arrived, so sitting on a kitchen floor by the light of the fridge was not necessarily new. What was new was the little pup nuzzling me and licking the shock-induced sweat from my brow.

When I began to feel better, I slowly stood and tested my blood again. It was getting closer to normal but still low. I grabbed my monitor and a banana and went to sit on a chair at the kitchen table, more confident that I would not pass out. As I sat and slowly ate, I finally started tasting the bitter adrenaline in my mouth that I had been too numb to notice previously. It made the banana taste weird, but I powered through. Besides becoming more and more awake, I was starting to feel better. I tested again and was normal.

"Thank you," I whispered to Geronimo, who was falling asleep in a ball by my feet. "You saved me, baby."

Tears welled in my eyes, and I instantly loved him with all my heart.

As I wigged my hand gently between his ears, massaging his furry head, I looked at the clock on the stove. It was only a little past two, so there was still enough time to sleep before my six o'clock alarm would disturb us.

"Com'on baby," I said, cooing Geronimo a little more awake.

I locked the back door and turned off the lights while my temporarily awakened pup followed every step. When we reached the room, he looked at me, anticipating I would pick him up and lock him in the crate. Instead, I picked him up and placed him on the foot of the bed. Within seconds, we were all asleep in our bed.

Bruce was surprised when he woke not only to an alarm but a bouncing baby fluffball. As I explained what had happened the night before, Bruce jostled and congratulated Geronimo with a thousand "good boys," cuddles, scratches and pets. From then on, Geronimo slept in bed with us every night. He also grew from a tiny pup who we needed to be lifted into bed, to our helping him jump up, to his being able to bound into bed in a single leap and take well more than his allotted sleep space.

Bruce's career was improving, and he was offered a job in an outback town. It paid well, and my PhD work was stalling due to supervisors resigning. I had also just started to undergo in vitro fertilization (IVF). With this, I found myself struggling to focus with the chemical rush of hormones, so a fresh start made sense. Plus, we needed the money—IVF is not inexpensive! Bruce flew ahead to start work, while I resigned from teaching at the college and from the PhD program with an advisor who didn't know me. I packed and cleaned out the house, then put Geronimo on a plane for Bruce to pick up at the airport in Emerald, Queensland. Lastly, I drove twenty-two hours over two days to our new rental house.

I liked this new, small town. Because the population was only around 1,000 residents, everyone seemed to know each other. In Sydney, I could hide, but in Tieri, I was the American wife and Geronimo's "mum." Between IVF treatments, I began tutoring children at the local school who needed help in reading and math. Geronimo settled in with this, allowing himself to be a footrest for the student I was helping to memorize multiplication tables or sound out tricky phonetic spellings. I was only grateful when my students brought Geronimo Christmas and birthday presents, forgetting me. And when I walked Geronimo around town to exercise both of us, school children I had never met called out, "Hi Geronimo!" which always made me smile.

"How do you know those kids?" I would ask him, but he only glanced at me with what I am sure was a grin, and never answered.

Bruce and I giggled at Geronimo's notoriety, and comfortably settled into small town life.

With a demanding, high-pressure job where he was the new guy, Bruce worked long hours, rarely taking time off. Geronimo was my close companion, driving with me to the grocery store and other errands. Because it was a small, crime-free town, and Geronimo was big and had a bark, I would leave him in the car with the key in the ignition and aircon running, especially when I was only dashing in for a few quick items.

"I saw Geronimo in the car," said neighbors as I collected medication from the pharmacy one afternoon, "so I knew you were both here doing errands."

This small talk blossomed into friendships, and friendships grew my confidence, so when Bruce and I decided to try IVF after our initial failure, we agreed that my driving to Sydney to stay with his parents was the best option. I would go through the medical prep, and he would fly in for a few days for the actual procedure.

Though *Paws for Diabetics* had just started in Australia, Geronimo was not a registered support dog. This fact did not deter me. Whenever I booked motels along our drive, I always noted that I had a "Diabetes support dog," opening all doors. I also felt more confident in Geronimo with me on those long drives in towns of which I was entirely unfamiliar. The lodgings always noted that he was supposed to sleep on the floor, but every night, my fluffy baby joined me in bed, just where he belonged. When I paused at rest stops, I brought him into the ladies' bathroom stalls with me, and when I bought a meal at fast food restaurants, I always ordered a side of bacon, just for him.

Geronimo was a great listener. He liked all the same music as me, and never complained about how fast or slow I was driving; I loved having him with me on those endless-feeling roads. I would stop every few hours to make sure he had water and could walk around to do his business, and I was grateful for these moments. These opportunities gave me a chance to fall in love with the Australian native landscape. I would take a moment and note the variations in soil and the changing native colours of the winding drive. I would breathe in the scents of various kinds of natural eucalyptuses that grow wildly along the length of the continent in almost every dusty path and lush roadway, inviting me to feel at home, even as an immigrant.

One time, when a last-minute, super-bargain round-trip flight to the US came up, I packed and left within 24 hours for a week in the US. While I was there, I ate burgers with American mustard, talked about Geronimo, bought him toys, and missed him. At home, he began misbehaving, even running away—just for a little while—from Bruce. Bruce was confused, still sure that Geronimo was "his" dog. But I knew the truth. Not wanting to hurt Bruce's feelings, I chorused his surprise.

When I came home, Geronimo snubbed me. Just turned up his nose and walked away, even huffing a bit. He was holding a grudge for my leaving him. I could see that he was sad, resenting that I had left without him, and he refused to look at me. I knelt down beside him, draping my arms around him.

"I am so sorry," I said. "That wasn't fair. You're a good dog. I love you. I missed you more than I missed Daddy." And then, as an afterthought, "but don't tell Daddy."

He sighed, nuzzled into me, and all was forgiven.

"Also, maybe this is our secret, that you're my dog, and not Daddy's," I added.

Geronimo smiled, and I knew he liked our secret.

Geronimo did not judge me when IVF did not work and loved me at a time when I was not sure I loved myself. He saw me cry more than anyone else in the world and only interrupted my thoughts and tears if my blood sugar began dipping too low, or to nudge me in his special way that I learned to trust, which meant he was saying, "I love you. It's okay. I'm here for you."

Geronimo began joining me when I went to visit nursing homes, making use of my idle and aimless time, and he made my gingerbread men disappear at Christmastime (naughty pup!). When a chocolate chip company advertised for customers to submit photos of their offspring to be added to the cover of a children's cookie cookbook, I sent in Geronimo's photo, mostly because I was feeling a little bit left out. But magically, a cookbook arrived, Geronimo's name and face on the cover. Bruce made copies, and we sent them to everyone on our Christmas card list. (I still have this cookbook.)

Bruce worked his way up, and soon we were moving again, this time for him to take a position in a corporate office in Brisbane, a city of over two million humans and plenty of dog parks. We signed up for a rental house that was adjacent to a dog-friendly beach. Geronimo was getting older, so I bought him a step to help him climb into our bed at night, and he would stay home when I went to the grocery store, or when Bruce and I attended a church on Sundays. Otherwise, he was by my side, joining me for twice or more daily walks along the beach, listening to me throw out ideas of what I should do with my childless life.

Supportive as always, Geronimo never judged me, no matter how crazy my ideas were. He followed me as I led him on long walks, as I stepped on the tangled, netted Mangrove tree roots, trying to avoid muddying my shoes, while Geronimo plopped alongside on, whatever path we might be on, never worrying about the mud, and only pausing to pull me to the ground if my blood sugar was too low for me to be safe to stand. It was at these moment that he nudged my bag open to the glucose tablets, raisins or juice boxes we always traveled with. I apologized to him when I had gel nails put on, not realizing I would not be able to scratch him as well as without the fake tips. As I peeled the heat-solidified, thick, sparkling chemical gel off, I promised him I would never, ever get gel or acrylic or any other kind of bogus nails done again. He cuddled up to me whenever he sensed I needed a hug, nudging me with his snout. I would rest my forehead on his, kissing his nose, telling him how much I loved him, how much I needed him, how grateful I was for him, how he filled a hole in my heart.

He played hide and seek with me, letting me hide with a dog treat, then only coming to find me when I called him. He barked at people with creepy vibes, protecting me from trespassers such as the common housefly and very suspicious postal workers delivering letters. He chased me as

I slid down the slide on the children's play equipment at a local park in the middle of the day, and jumped in after me every time I went into a swimming pool, then lazily required me to hold him while he cooled off and relaxed in the water. And every night I slept, feeling safe that he was by my side, both when Bruce was home and when Bruce was away for work.

As Halloween rolled around yet another year, I timidly agreed to attend the church trunk-or-treat. Without children, I was not very comfortable at the family-oriented church social activities, but I did love Halloween. And being even more of an outlier, I liked candy corn—a lot. Always have. Candy disguised as an actual food such as corn always appealed to the misbehaving diabetic child inside of me. Placing this candy corn sin aside, I prepped a plastic cauldron with dozens of mini chocolate bars while Bruce marked where in white sheet to cut eye and snout holes for Geronimo's ghost costume. Geronimo wasn't sure what was going on, but he was ready for whatever we were doing! Sitting in the hatchback of our midsize SUV that we decorated with battery-operated purple and orange twinkling lights, Geronimo sat panting and smiling while dozens of children helped themselves to candy from the cauldron. And at the end of the night, when the prize for the best costume was announced, Geronimo was declared the winner! We were duly proud of our boy.

We decided to buy a house again, and purchased one we could afford, a handful of miles from the dog beach, but close enough to go back for regular visits. And then—suddenly, magically, after ten years of marriage and eight years of dog parenting, we were able to adopt two children. It was our eighth Christmas with Geronimo, our cards included a photo of our daughters alongside our dog. But that would be the last.

Geronimo wasn't walking as well as usual, and he seemed in pain. I wondered if it was the new weight of toddlers wrestling on top of him or something else? After initial, and then multiple visits to various veterinarians, I could not deny the diagnosis: Bone cancer. Hearing the diagnosis, I sobbed with uncontrollable belly gulps, lamenting deeper in my soul than with any other loss before. Or since. The treatment, which was a serious gamble, was deeply, painfully cruel. I could never ask him to go through that for me.

Geronimo was dying, and he did not have much time. Within weeks, he was barely about to walk, and mostly dragged himself from place to place. I would take the children to daycare twice a week, and on those sacred, fleeting days, I would drive Geronimo along the beach, parking as close as we could get to the sea so he could smell the salt air and we could breathe in our shared memories. I would weep and talk of the old days with him, wishing myself back in time, regretting the moments of years past when he asked me to throw a stick into the water another time but I wouldn't, too much in a hurry or lost in my own thoughts about what I wanted rather than celebrating what I had. He never complained, neither about the lack of stick throwing, nor that I was not strong enough to carry him closer to sea.

I was not ready for him to go. But it was time. He could

no longer walk and would lay in his filth until I cleaned him. I always told him I didn't mind, that every extra second was worth it. But Geronimo wasn't well. He could no longer climb stairs or jump in our bed, so I took to sleeping on the floor by him, this time without complaint. Finally, Bruce put his foot down. And I knew he was right.

We drove our boy to the animal hospital for the appointment. The veterinarians and staff were gentle and loving, with us and our fur child. Medicine was administered, first to cause him to relax, and then fall asleep.

With reverence, but all too soon, the vet tenderly spoke, "He's gone." She excused herself, inviting us to "take your time."

After a moment, Bruce left, telling me he would be in the car, but not to hurry. I knew he needed a moment to cry privately.

I pressed my forehead against Geronimo's, snuggling my nose alongside his snout. That was the way we communicated that we loved each other, free from words. I kept rubbing his head, wishing for him to look at me, but knowing he would not. I kissed my son—because he was my son—and whispered, "I love you." I closed my eyes and envisioned Geronimo bouncing and playfully running into the arms of my father, who had passed away when I was a teen. The sun was shining, and my dad took the stick from Geronimo and threw it... and before long, they were both playing fetch much too far away from me to imagine anymore. I kissed him again and said goodbye.

Before Geronimo, I thought that true love was amorous: that it was a romantic relationship that would keep my heart safe and love me through thick and thin. And mostly, Bruce fills that part. But true, unconditional love—I learned that through Geronimo. Prior to my fur baby, I could never imagine how much love he brought, as well as protection with his powerful bark and his amazing ability to sense my blood sugars. He gave me confidence to drive long distances in the outback—on the left side of the road—and stay in motels in towns I had never been to before or since. He kept me company where I was lonely, listened to all of my thoughts and fears, forgave me, and never judged me. It is not just chance that the levidrome of d-o-g is g-o-d. A dog's love is perfect and teaches us how to live and love with superb and overwhelming purity.

Geronimo both parented and protected me, and allowed me to parent him. Through him, I learned patience, loyalty, forgiveness, and he taught me to feel love at times when I felt like I did not deserve it. He missed me when I was gone, and greeted me at the door as though the 30 seconds it took me to roll out the garbage bin was as distant and durative as being sent off to war for years. In him, I experienced both giving and receiving unconditional love. Words truly cannot express the depth of this feeling.

A decade after Geronimo's passing, I was visiting with my elderly, widowed, pet-loving aunt, and chatting about family who had passed away. In that decade, Bruce and I adopted another dog, and then another, both who were his dogs, likely because I was more focused on our children.

As my aunt and I talked about what heaven might be like, I mindlessly spoke, "I personally, don't care about seeing people in the next life. I just want to see my dog."

"Me, too!" she said, surprising me. Then looking at me intently, she reaffirmed, "Me, too. About seeing my dogs in heaven. Humans come and go. But the love from a dog is eternal."

I was too teary to speak, sharing a wordless moment of understanding the genuine love that comes from our soul mates who wear waggy tails, floppy ears, and have perpetually open hearts. Fur love is forever love. I know this with all my heart.

ELEVEN

Old Dog at Night
JOHN SAVOIE

The old dog mewls at the back door
frozen shut—I cannot open it
to show him there's nothing
out there—and so he moans
like the humpback whale
spinning slowly on its flukes
six hundred feet deep amid
the blackest blue, pearling
the abyss with spiral song
rising into a congeries of stars
spun from their dark center,
notes lonely and pure as the last
castrato soaring the silent night,
silence that seems as cruel then
as now, in this dog's last December.
But look how he pauses and tilts
his head to listen, then begins

again, as if he were the one
answering the song that is
already there, hidden among
the secret frequencies, melos
quiet as the fern tingling
its green fingers in April rain
as the dead earth wakes once more.
And so the old dog whimpers
and keens and sometimes simply
stares in sympathy with the sad
beautiful things of this world
for which I lack, for which he has,
the softest silken ears to hear.

TWELVE

The Gift

TIM KELLER

My Mother usually began her Christmas shipping in June, but this year, she announced she would no longer buy presents for all the children, grandchildren, and great-grandchildren. Instead, she would take down Dad's life story and use the installments as gifts for the family.

Secretly, I and everyone else in the family considered this something of a holiday foul, but the folks are long retired now, and as the family has grown, the time and expense of shopping for everyone had become prohibitive. So, we all smiled and nodded politely.

Only I suspected the fullness of the implication—that Mom would nag Dad until he finally deigned to speak. She would then write his every utterance in longhand until her arthritic fingers could take no more and leave the resulting hieroglyphs for me to decipher.

When she brought me the notebook to transcribe, it was

all I could do not to groan. Except for a list of titles ("My First Horse," "My Trip to the Dentist," "The Old Yellow School House"), the pad was empty. I realized that, in addition to my own holiday and writing responsibilities, I could now look forward to—this.

Mom must have read the frustration in my expression because her next words were: "Your father is a great man."

It's a familiar refrain. What's more, it's true. Stalwart and glacially calm, his moral compass reliable as true north, Dad's an exemplar of his generation. But though I love him dearly, we've rarely seen eye to eye.

See, Dad was born a middle-aged conservative who took his seat on the high council the moment he left the womb. I, on the other hand, am impulsive and ruled by passion. We get along all right around other people, but alone, we're sort of like two old tomcats circling in an alley.

"I know," I assured her. "It's just...do you want to write it down for me?" I asked hopefully. "Then I could, you know, edit it. That way it would sound more like Dad was doing the telling."

"No," said Mom. "I want you to give it some style. You know, write it like one of your books or something."

Wonderful, I thought, pulling out my laptop. *The gift that keeps on taking.*

"Yeah," Dad said with an amused snort. "Style me up."

"Dear," said Mom in that special tone of hers, the one that says *proceed at your peril*. "I know you think this is silly, but I'm sure your children and grandchildren think otherwise. Besides, it will save us over two thousand dollars in gifts this year alone. So, you can take this seriously, or you can break out the checkbook and start writing."

I started up the laptop, sat on the sofa facing Dad's easy chair, and waited, smiling.

Mom had us trapped, and we knew it. Dad grunted a begrudging affirmative, cleared his throat, and began to speak.

I grew up during the Great Depression, and my family was large, even by the standard of the day. Then again, people didn't worry about things like that back then. Yes, more kids meant more mouths to feed, but they also meant more help around the farm. Families took care of each other in those days, you see.

With four older brothers and four older sisters, I was the baby of the family. Which meant that Mother and my sisters spoiled me rotten, while the older boys had to do the heavy farm work. The only bad part was that everything I owned used to belong to someone else! I got two new pairs of pants a year—a church pair on Christmas and Levis on my birthday. Everything else was a hand-me-down, including my horse.

Buttons became mine by default. She was too old to carry anyone else in the family, but I was only six years old at the time. I couldn't lift the saddle to put on her, nor could I reach her head to bridle her, but to the family's amazement, I'd simply call, and over the fence she'd come. I would give her some oats, climb the fence, slip onto her back, and off we'd go.

This went on until my mother saw. That's when Papa (at Mama's insistence) taught me how wrap a rope around Buttons' head and neck. Just like that, I was the only boy in all of Mink Creek, Idaho with his very own horse. She would take me over Devil's Hill to Grandma Christensen's for a cookie, or over the dip to the hot springs for a swim with my buddies.

We were just little kids, but folks didn't worry like they do today, and our parents all knew—old Buttons looked out for us. Like the time my friend Arlen told us they had baby geese at their place and we should all come see. His daddy admonished him to leave them alone, but they were only birds. So, we rode Buttons over to his place and slid off her to see the geese.

"They can already swim," he told me.

Of course, I didn't believe him. Surely, they were too young.

"They can!" he insisted. "Help me chase 'em to the creek, and I'll prove it."

So, we rounded 'em up and were headin 'em to the creek when the mother geese turned and came at us. Their necks stretched forward, beating wings outstretched, and they honked so loud it hurt our ears. The lead one flew up and grabbed my nose, beating me with its wings. I started screaming. I thought they were going to kill us.

Old Buttons came charging to the rescue. Her first pass sent geese and feathers flying everywhere. She stood between them and us and reared up, beating the air with her hooves. It was an awesome sight for us little kids.

The geese beat a hasty retreat, and they were the last geese I ever bothered. Word got around though, and suddenly we were famous.

Buttons was as faithful a companion as a boy ever had, but as I grew up, her coat grew spotty, and she developed a deep bow in her back. A pure-bred quarter horse, she'd once been the fastest in the territory. Now she could barely lope. Buttons was still a great friend, but she was no longer fancy, not to a bunch of eleven-year-olds no longer afraid of geese (not much anyway).

So, Buttons and I went from famous to infamous, though anyone who said as much could (and often did) end up with a black eye, and much as I loved her, even I had to admit she was an old nag. I begged my father for another horse, a real horse, maybe even a thoroughbred. But it was the Depression. We had workhorses and Buttons. My brothers had to ride the workhorses, Dad reminded me. He said I should be grateful, and I knew he was right. If I wanted a horse of my own, I'd have to find a way to get it myself.

I wracked my brain trying to figure that one out. I was heartsick. I had five dollars saved up, but I wanted a horse like the one I saw at the county fair that summer. The old Johnson ranch got foreclosed on that year. A California dude bought it and started trucking in livestock. The first time any of us ran into him was at the fair, where he showed up with King, the most magnificent horse I'd ever laid eyes on. Horses like that went for hundreds of dollars and more, even in those days.

King was an enormous white stallion, both good-natured and fast! He passed all the locals like they were standing still. What with my appreciation for fine horse flesh, seeing that animal made it all worse. There was no way I could afford even a regular horse, much less a magnificent steed like him. I was already managing all the work I could fit into a day, doing chores and hauling hay at home, then doing odd jobs for the neighbors.

I worked and prayed, and prayed and worked, and as happens when you do your part, inspiration came.

That night at dinner, I asked Papa, "If I can find a way to get my own horse, can I keep him?"

My brothers all laughed at me, and I turned red, but I was determined to have my answer.

"Sounds fair to me, " he said as Mama hushed my brothers up.

I set to work the very next day.

The Anderson family ran a big dairy back then, and their land bordered the old Johnson place. This was before milking machines, and the cows had to be milked twice a day. No one wanted to work at the dairy. It was hot and dirty work, especially in the summer. So, when I asked Mr. Anderson if he needed any help, he hired me on the spot, leaving only Mama to convince. She seemed to sense the urgency of my need and, to my great surprise, even let me out of church for the whole summer!

It was hard work all right. Every day I rode Buttons over the Anderson's before first light and led her up the hill to the pasture.

It wasn't too bad in the morning. The cows would be

waiting patiently by the barn door, and the family of cats we'd give the occasional squirt of milk lined the wall. We'd run the cows in, two at a time, milk 'em, dump the bucket into the milk cans, run 'em out again, and do two more. I'd go back up between milkings to get Buttons, ride home to do chores there, and then ride back up.

The afternoon milking was a different story. We had to fight the cows, the heat, and the flies. Even the cats'd be gone. The hotter the day, the thicker the flies, and when the cows couldn't swish them off fast enough with their tails, they'd head for the creek and run through the brush to get 'em off. Then Buttons and I'd have to ride down there and drive 'em back.

Come Friday, I'd get paid a whole five dollars for the week. I was too tired to ever spend it, but it wasn't the money I was after anyhow. Fall rolled around, and back to school and church I went. Every morning, I rushed through my chores so I could sneak Buttons some extra oats or apples and carrots from Mama' kitchen.

By Thanksgiving, old Buttons had a certain glow about her. By Christmas, she was downright fat, and my brothers, Paul and Roland, the businessmen of the family, were suspicious. One day they stood by the pasture fence arguing over whether Buttons could be pregnant and vying for the colt in case she was.

"She's my horse," I reminded them.

Which didn't seem to matter to them at all.

"We're older," Ronald said. "You can have Old Nick."

They had a good laugh at that. Old Nick was a fat old

Clydesdale, great for pulling loads but so wide at the middle his rider's legs all but did the splits.

"Hell, that horse ain't pregnant," Paul opined, chewing on a piece of straw. "She's just fat."

"Thing's ready for the glue factory if she ain't," Roland said.

That made my blood boil. My plan, all my hard work—I could feel it all slipping away. Much to my shame, my eyes started to water.

"She's my horse, and it's my colt!" I shouted.

They laughed again.

"What you gonna do, Baby Boy?" Roland asked, using Mama's name for me, and gave me a shove. "Cry?"

We'd always been taught to love each other, and we really did, but ashamed as I am to admit it, in that moment, I hated him.

"She's mine!" I screamed jumping on his back.

Roland was seventeen and real strong, but I wrapped my legs around him, sank my teeth into his neck, and held on for dear life.

He shook and bucked and bellered like a rodeo bronc until Paul pried me off.

Roland jumped up and looked to come after me, but a single, particularly expressive snort from Buttons bought me a head start. I ran blubbering into the house and hid in my room. Mad and embarrassed, Roland gave chase, but Mama met him at the door while my sister Velma followed me to my room.

I broke down at her urging and told her the story.

How I'd rode Buttons over to the Anderson's in the

mornings, and pastured her right next to the old Johnson place. Once there, I simply unhooked the fence wires to let Buttons in with King.

The look on Velma's face made me suddenly very nervous. I'd grown up on stories about how they shot horse thieves on sight, and while this wasn't the same, I knew it wasn't exactly right, either.

"What?" I asked. "She had to eat too, didn't she? It wasn't stealing exactly. I mean, King was the one who took care of business, after all."

Velma laughed, and I knew I'd be okay.

"Before long, Buttons had a boyfriend," I continued. "And when she started kicking at King a few weeks later, I knew the deed was done."

Velma called Mama, and I'd just gotten through relating the story to her when Papa, Paul, and a disheveled Roland came in.

"Why did you bite your brother?" Papa growled.

Mama met him, hands on hips. "Adam Archibald Keller!"

She rarely called my father by name, and in my whole life, I'd never heard her use all three; it certainly got his attention.

"That mare is his, and that colt is his! You gave him your word, and that's one promise I aim to make sure you keep!"

Not to be outdone, Papa shouted, "Has this whole danged family gone nuts? Good hell woman, that thing's 'bout as pregnant as I am."

You could hardly blame him. It's not every day you see a twenty-five-year-old mare on a farm full of geldings catch pregnant. I mean, talk about immaculate conception.

"Then you'd better stock up on saltines and hot towels," Mama replied, "because Leness has a story to tell you."

By the time I was done, order had been restored and everyone was in good spirits. Everyone but Roland anyhow, and even he settled down, eventually. Papa made me go see Mr. Johnson, who'd stayed on as ranch foreman. I admitted what I'd done and had to work for him every day of Christmas vacation, but I didn't mind.

On a blustery April afternoon, Buttons gave birth to the most beautiful little filly I've seen before or since. She was light Palomino with a star on her head and four stocking feet. Between me, Buttons, and my sisters, no horse was ever loved more. The girls called her Kate, but being a boy, I called her Skyrocket.

Buttons died peacefully a couple of years later, and Papa died of cancer a year after that. The sale of Skyrocket's foals helped us keep the family farm. Years later, I said a tearful goodbye to Skyrocket as we sold her to pay for my mission to Georgia. Mama never told anyone, but she put what she didn't use into savings bonds, and when I got back from Korea, she cashed them out to help with our house.

I typed furiously, trying to capture the moment, when I realized the room had gone quiet. Only the whir of the fan on my laptop and the ticking of the clock could be heard. I looked up to find Dad staring off into space, his eyes moist.

"Wait, Skyrocket?" I asked. "You called Queenie Skyrocket, and Kate before her."

"Every horse since Buttons," he said.

Then he picked up the newspaper and I could tell we were done.

I gazed at him like a stranger. There sat my father, an old and honorable man to be sure, but for the first time, I also saw a twelve-year-old boy, sneaking his ancient mare through a hole in a fence.

THIRTEEN

Pets Are for Kids

DAVID S. TAYLOR

The nature of pet ownership has changed over my life's span—personally and in general. As a kid, I enjoyed growing up with a dog for a pal. When I was young, pets were mainly for kids. Only a few of the kids in my neighborhood had pet dogs, and cats numbered even fewer. Nowadays, I see more and more adults walking multiple dogs or housing multiple cats. In our neighborhood, there's even a guy who walks his cat on a leash. First time I've seen that!

Looking at past generations, pet ownership changes stand out even more dramatically. Back then, dogs fulfilled more roles than companionship. On the farm, they kept predators away and helped herd the sheep. Cats reduced the mouse population. Animals mostly took care of themselves and stayed outside year-round. Now, dogs and cats are members of the family, sharing living spaces with children and parents.

Pet attitudes pass from generation to generation and

intersect with in-law relationships. My wife grew up with small indoor dogs; my childhood dog stayed outside. Late in our marriage, we tried an indoor kitten for a while until it tore up the carpet and a folding door. Two of our four children owned indoor pets for their kids, one with multiple cats and one with a well-trained Golden Retriever. Our other two children, influenced by our family's experiences, allergies, and their spouses' traditions, elected to forego the commitment and trouble of keeping pets.

Pets—commitment and trouble? Children may beg their parents for a pet and promise to take care of it. However, when the novelty wears off, parents end up assuming more and more of the responsibility for feeding, walking, and cleaning up after the animal. Then family vacations require arrangements for pet care—ball and chain? However, people who think pets are for adults don't seem to mind. The companionship of animal family members seems to outweigh the extra effort. I still think pets are for kids.

My dad acquired Queenie for my growing-up pet. He hoped she would also act as a pheasant hunting dog, but I think he found I did better at systematically flushing the birds along a fence line. The dog wandered randomly and acted surprised when she sniffed out a pheasant.

Queenie was a mild-mannered, Boxer-type crossbreed. She wore the colors of a Boxer, fawn body with white chest and black snout, and had a bobbed tail but no pug nose. I know dogs don't have human facial expressions, but it seemed like Queenie's eyebrows always projected a hopeful look, reinforced by her vigorously wagging stub of a tail. No matter how much I ignored her, she always volunteered as my ready companion. Her greetings sent warmth radiating through my body. However, her short, stiff hair resembled small, pointed, porcupine quills, and if I hugged her with bare arms, the fur raised little welts in my skin. Petting the dog at arm's length with the palms of my hands avoided that problem.

I loved Queenie and didn't mind taking care of her—when I remembered. I suspect part of my parents' reason for the pet was to teach me responsibility. That daily feeding ritual now brings memories of the meaty smell of her dog food contained in cans with bright red labels. It seemed feeding time provided Queenie with the best part of her day.

When playing in the backyard or going to a friend's house, I could let Queenie loose from her cage. Most of the time, however, she remained penned up. Sadly for her, my playing with friends took priority over playing with the dog.

"Can Terry come out and play?"

"Sorry, he has to do his chores."

"Can Steve come out and play?"

"Sorry, we're taking him shopping today."

With drooped shoulders, I contemplated a boring Saturday morning. Then I hitched up my shoulders again and ran home to Queenie. I knew she'd be waiting and ready.

Queenie was gentle with us kids, and I only heard her bark once. When I became an uncle at age eight, she didn't seem to mind my little nieces handling her. Yet we never thought of allowing her into our house.

Like me, Salt Lake City, where I grew up, was younger and less sophisticated in those days. The simpler life there held fewer people, fewer dogs, and fewer cars. A leash was optional for walking your dog, and we never heard or thought of picking up droppings.

One evening, on a walk with my father and Queenie, as we approached an intersection, our unleashed dog darted after a prize into the street in front of an oncoming car. Dad and I panicked in chorus!

"Queenie!" we screamed in harmony.

She jumped back just in time, but not before snatching the trophy of her sniffing focus, a paper-wrapped hamburger. In her excitement, she swallowed the whole thing in one gulp—wrapper and all! My heart beat fast, and I wiped my brow at the close call. Then I wondered how much she enjoyed the burger. For years afterward, Dad and I laughed about Queenie's hasty meal—real "fast food!"

Queenie got lost once. She wandered off from my Little League baseball game. I missed my dog, worried about her, and wondered if I would ever see her again. A week later, my parents drove me home from ball practice. As I gazed aimlessly out the backseat window, I spotted our lost dog on someone's porch.

"There's Queenie!" I shouted.

Before the car stopped completely, I leapt from the backseat and ran across the street toward her. She spotted me, her ears perked up, and she ran toward me. I embraced her, and she licked me. Joyful reunion of boy and dog with hugging, despite the welts!

Years later, it saddened me when my boyhood playmate

had to be put down due to age and cancer. No longer in childhood, I sojourned 1,800 miles away from home and Queenie, serving as a missionary for the Church of Jesus Christ of Latter-day Saints in Tennessee. My parents inherited the responsibility of taking care of my pet in my absence. They offered me the option to keep our dog alive until I returned home. I faced a difficult decision. If Dad took care of the euthanasia, Queenie wouldn't suffer longer, and I would be spared the pain of taking her to her fate. I thought the distance would make our parting easier. Still, it hurt that I couldn't say goodbye. We would not have another joyful, boy-and-dog reunion until after this life.

In our married life, we experimented with owning pets—for the sake of our four children.

Allie-Boo, the outdoor black-and-white cat, born of a stray mother in a woodpile on an Idaho farm, had a rough beginning. At our house in Smithfield, she acted stand-offish and neurotic—not what I considered a warm pet. One of our sons recalls she was hard to corner.

"Are you my pet?" he would ask her.

One day, while my wife ran errands, she noticed strange, squeaky noises from the front of the car. She pulled over and popped the hood. No squeak and nothing out of the ordinary. The squeak persisted off and on throughout the day. Acting on a hunch, she stopped by a vet.

"It sounds more like an animal noise than an engine

noise," she told the vet. "Besides, I hear it sometimes when I turn off the engine."

"Well, I've never done auto repair at my clinic before, but I'll have a look," he said.

In the parking lot, two heads leaned in and searched the engine compartment.

"There it is!" he said as he pulled out a black-and-white, screeching furball from its hiding place in the corner.

Allie-Boo had endured a frenetic, stop-and-go joy ride all over the valley in her precarious hiding place. When my wife told me about it, I shuddered in sympathy but still couldn't bond with Allie-Boo. I was busy earning a living for the family.

Our other son, the one who ended up as a cat owner, liked Allie-Boo. He took the time and effort to round her up and pet her.

"Coming home from school, it warmed me all over to hear and feel her purr," he told me.

Maybe that's why, as a parent, he procured a separate cat for each of his three daughters.

This son also said, "Dogs forgive, but cats remember."

Perhaps that's why Allie-Boo and I didn't hit it off.

Allie-Boo did stay around our house and in strange ways acted like she belonged to our family, like putting paw prints all over our parked cars. And whenever we drove into our long driveway, the cat would appear out of nowhere and demonstrably strut over to her food dish. Also, she often deposited dead mice and birds on our porch. Was that her way of showing affection? I appreciated her execution as a mouser, but why did she leave her trophies where we might step on them? Coming from a farm as she did, she would have made a great pet for the previous generation.

Because Allie-Boo stayed outside, she didn't bother me too much, except whenever she tried to sneak into the house. Mostly, we coexisted. One time, stealthily snuck in and forgotten, she shredded the curtain sheers on the inside of our front room windows. That perturbed my wife, ruining her previous endearment toward the cat.

Concurrent with Allie-Boo, we owned an outside dog named "Pup," a tan-and-white Brittany Spaniel. Like typical dog owners, we kept her in our backyard. Pup was not silent like Queenie, but I trained her to stop barking when I hollered:

"Quiet!"

In lieu of a pen, Pup lived on the end of a 20-foot chain, staked so she could reach her doghouse. She left her droppings on one half of her circle. Our kids called it "the minefield." Upon looking back, they expressed regret for not playing with her more.

"We took her for granted," our oldest son admitted. After keeping an inside dog for his kids for 16 years, he said, "I should have brushed Pup more and scooped up the minefield."

He became a new-generation pet person. Yet, when their dog died, he did not replace her with another pet.

"When the novelty for the kids wears off," he told me, "The parents have to pick up the slack. It can be burdensome, and I had to neglect our pet to focus on raising the children. Looking back, I have more regrets than happy memories."

However, he and his siblings do have fond memories of Pup in their childhoods.

"It was fun to take Pup on hikes," he said.

"I loved that she let you hug her," his brother told me.

"I liked to pet and talk to her," said our daughter.

"She was always excited to see you," our youngest said.

As our children matured, they got busy and had less time for Pup. Her only company most of the time was Allie-Boo. The cat would sit by the doghouse with Pup, seeming to bond more with the dog than with us. But I wondered if Allie-Boo was truly being friendly or just lording her freedom over the dog.

And Pup loved any freedom she could garner. In our kids' younger years, they would let her off her chain when playing in the backyard. Then their games distracted them until one of them would say:

"Where's Pup?" And off they'd go to search the neighborhood!

Time passed, the kids grew up, and I became the main one to take her for walks. Wait! Weren't pets supposed to be for the kids?

I didn't mind the walks though; they gave me exercise.

I think our dog lived for our walks. When I came toward the doghouse carrying the leash, Allie-Boo skedaddled, and Pup started jumping up and down on her chain, anxious for a walk.

I'm pretty sure our kids became more attached to our pets than I did, but their passings tore at my heartstrings. One winter evening, my wife looked out from her basement sewing room window and discovered Allie-Boo curled up and lifeless in the window well. Her unanticipated death sent a wave of sorrow over us.

Pup's end was also sad, though not unforeseen. She contracted pneumonia.

"This pill will either cure her or kill her," the vet told us.

She didn't survive it. Her body was too large to bury in the garden like we did with the cat, so the vet disposed of her. This time, distance didn't spare me the pain of taking my walking partner to her fate.

Since humans live longer than animals, children can learn about death from their pets. Backyard funerals prepare them for losses of loved ones. Our teenage granddaughter's heart broke when her only pet, a betta fish named "Salty," passed away.

Over time, dogs and cats have come a long way from barnyard accessories to intimate family members. In our neighborhood at least, it seems they've morphed from devices for teaching kids responsibility to recipients of adult pampering. In some cases, pets take the place of children in a family, especially for empty nesters. These days, veterinarians and pet stores thrive with booming businesses. Walkers of dogs carry little green plastic bags for you know what. I'm sure some pets are still taken for granted, but in general, most are better off in our refined urban society.

I share my children's regrets for neglecting my childhood pet. If I could go back, I would have spent more time with Queenie. My heart has soft spots for Queenie, Pup, and even

Allie-Boo. But for me, there's something special in the wonder of being a kid and having a pet. Our second son expressed it:

"I'm grateful to my parents for letting me have pets as a kid."

Personally, now, I'm all in as an empty nester—I don't have to find babysitters or pet sitters for our vacations. I prefer not to scoop poop and deal with hair all over the house.

Don't get me wrong. I don't hate animals, though I am barking intolerant. In fact, I enjoy watching trained, well-behaved pets—with paws and claws, fur, wet noses, and drooling tongues kept at a respectable distance. I delight in watching our one-year-old great-grandson and his pet-buddy Artemis, a jet-black cat, romp together. But please don't ask me to cuddle a cat or dog. I might sneeze or get a rash.

With the children gone, I have no need for a pet. I'm perfectly happy to go walking on my own or with my wife—providing the neighborhood dogs behave. So, in the end, we two older adults remain pet-less. And I like it that way.

FOURTEEN

When It Rains in Spain

ANNE STARK

Spanish pop music icon Joaquin Sabina has a hit called "Llueve Sobre Mojada" which literally means, "It's raining on top of wet." That was the kind of rain we had on a spring morning in Mojácar, Spain.

It was a massive, gutter-cleansing rain over the white adobe apartment we were renting for a few months during our sabbatical. Determined to take my morning jog despite Sabina's "raining over wetness," I faced off in the direction of the sea, about a mile away by crow's flight and five hundred feet elevation drop. The Mediterranean Sea often appeared in eight shades of teal and aqua, but today it was a solid slate color, deep and angry-looking.

My husband and I were spending the spring researching and writing on Spain's Costa de la Luz ("The Coast of Light"). Our Spanish was improving by the day, but we didn't speak it much to each other at home. We sprinkled the occasional *vale* ("okay") or *claro* ("for sure") into our conversation, and some Spanglish, like "exactamundo," meaning, "that's exactly right." On some late mornings, we might cue up Latin music on the playlist, including Eddie Palmieri's "Café," with whom we agreed the coffee was perfectly toasted ("tosta'o y cola'o"). Despite our idyllic conditions for work and relationship building, I was having trouble fitting into the community, especially with Spanish women. I struggled at the supermarket, knowing which produce I should touch and which vegetables I could bag myself without being scolded by a raven-haired woman much younger that I was.

That morning, I kicked open a rusty iron gate and wandered over a terra-cotta terrace rimmed with Moorish tile, then skipped down 227 limestone steps until I intersected with a concrete alley and two more uneven staircases. This was a formidable workout for a 63-year-old, even without the rain. But I safely reached the village of old town Mojácar.

After passing by the few cafés and newsstands, I made the right turn onto a lane called Las Casas Rurales, featuring a rural neighborhood of freestanding homes, unlike the packed-in apartments of the city. Jogging on the wet pavement, I almost ran over two dogs scampering in the middle of the road. They were so small they both could fit into a medium-sized Salt Lake City shoulder bag. Their fur was matted flat to their bodies as they meandered back and forth over the cracked asphalt. Despite the danger of being roadkill, the dogs frolicked like best pals. One was a golden orange Pomeranian, the other a ball of wet, brown fur that I took for a mutt.

Shoulders on this road were non-existent, jagged rock rising precipitously. This was a landscape where rock-scape and wildflowers spoke of an idyllic space untouched by developers. Besides the risk of cars and falls, this was not a friendly environment for two small dogs. Who knew when these pups last had a meal?

I cornered the vagrants against boulders to scoop them up and protect them from imminent death. The mutts immediately soaked through my jogging jacket. Searching through their matted coats, I found no tags, but after they stopped squirming in my arms, they rested comfortably together, as if they were from the same household.

With my smelly armful in tow, I trudged back toward town. A small path opened to beach homes, with fenced-in, angry canines of various sizes. I searched for open gates.

For a happy brand of people, Spaniards emote their anger easily, as I found whenever I was waiting in line in what's called a "cola," or tail. As was the case with touching certain types of vegetables at the market, I'd born criticism for butting ahead in a snaggle-tailed cola more than once. My fear of getting involved was enhanced the last time I meddled with a Spanish poodle owner whose dog tried to bite me. The owner snarled at me and hissed, "You scared him!" But I was a slow learner.

Confident that despite the menacing clouds above me, my efforts were going to have a positive outcome, I headed up the hill into the mist of mid-morning. I found a man hauling rocks in a wheelbarrow and explained my situation in halting Spanish. Shaking his head, he scoffed.

"They're not mine," he said as he returned to his gardening. "Can't help you, honey."

I followed a road into a cul-de-sac where each home stood shut up tight as a safe. At the door of one house, a woman emerged in a long housecoat. In my arms, the dogs grew heavier, more bovine than canine.

The young woman took the shaggier one in her arms. "I don't recognize them," she told me, "but I will ask around."

She tried to hand the dog back to me, but I shook my head. "Isn't there an animal shelter around here?" I asked.

"Not sure. They're really cute. But I'm sorry, I have to get ready for work," she said.

She agreed to hold the Pomeranian while I searched Google for a shelter. I located a place called "PAWS Patas," with, remarkably, the same acronym as the shelter in my hometown in Northern Utah. Small animal lover world, I thought. Unfortunately, the shelter was located in the newer subdivision of rich Brit and European ex-pats called Mojácar Playa, a full half-mile away.

Saying goodbye to the woman in the robe, I reclaimed the Pomeranian and headed south toward the beach. With the two scruff-muffins in my arms, I lumbered into the new village.

I was surprised to find my British friend Esther in a parking lot, closing the hatch of her mini-SUV. Her three mastiffs wove around in the back like a mighty boa constrictor. Juggling my squirming deadweights, I explained my situation once again, this time in English. She knew of PAWS Patas, but looked skeptical.

"My puppies are in the back, and I cahn't leave them for long," she said.

"But I'm about to drop one of these guys."

"Right-ee-o." Esther took the Pomeranian from me and turned over its paw. "Shite, their nails have not been clipped. They've been on their own for quite some time."

"How've they survived?"

"Finding food and water somewhere." Esther exhaled her a cigarette-tinged breath. "Listen, I'll wahlk with you over to the shelter."

Each of us holding a pup, we reached a newer building with large windows, and Esther frowned. "As I suspected. A thrift store. They don't house animals here."

"What?"

"Sorry, my friend. I gottah go rescue my lovies." She passed me back the orange, wet Nerf ball.

Shouldering the hapless creatures, I entered the place, where racks of used clothes separated women chatting in Spanish.

The clerks oohed and ahhed over the strays.

"We can't keep them here," said the main clerk. "We're only a charity for the main shelter in Turre."

"But that's fifteen kilometers! And your website—"

"Sorry. We'll call over there, and Cristina will come and pick them up. It'll take about an hour."

"But I need to get back; I haven't had breakfast, and—" I readjusted my grip as the main clerk called Cristina.

"One's a male, the other's a female," she whispered into

her phone, then she turned to me and said, "Maybe you can find a couple of belts to use as a leash...there's a sale on belts."

"Here's a soft one," another clerk offered. "You can loop it around this fellow's neck."

Their harnesses secured, the female dog lapped up a long drink from a bowl of water, but when I showed the bowl to the male, he leapt out of his bounds and scampered into the parking lot. Outside, he made feints between cars like an American running back. Realizing that my chasing him only made his scurry into danger, I held back.

He raced toward the thoroughfare, El Paseo del Mediteráneo, where cars careened around the little pooch, but somehow he crossed the street successfully and disappeared into the bushes. I trudged back to the thrift store empty-handed, where the customers passed the shaggy female back and forth.

"She's a Brussels Griffon!" one of them declared. "Worth a lot of money." *Un monton de dinero.* "Here, take her, and we'll look for the other one."

"Hey, I'll look for him on my way home," I said.

"*Vale,*" the main clerk replied sadly. Reluctantly, they agreed to watch the Brussels Griffon until Cristina showed up.

As I trudged back up the hill, looking around rocks and under bushes for a bundle of orange fur, I grew sadder by the minute. Two hours earlier, the survivors, while wet and unkempt, had been enjoying themselves. Now they were separated forever. I retraced the 227 stair-steps.

Slamming the metal door of our apartment, I slunk into a

kitchen chair. A text from my husband asked me to join him at a café, but I wasn't hungry anymore.

Hours later, my phone rang. Cristina from the animal shelter in Turre.

"You're a hero," she said in greeting. *Una heroina.*

"What?"

"We found the Pomeranian. And we also found someone to take the Brussels Griffon. An elderly woman, rich, homebound, will adopt her if no one claims her. That dog's feet will never have to touch ground if she doesn't want to."

"But who will take the other one? The male."

"Don't worry, we'll find someone. You did the right thing, picking them up off the road. It's a shame we don't have a shelter in Mojácar. We have to rely on responsible people like you."

Wow. Okay then. Praise from a Spaniard, a Spanish woman no less.

I thanked her, ending the call from a higher plane. Later, I found out someone from the store did indeed take the Pomeranian because neither of the dogs were chipped. With breeds like that, why wouldn't the owners have microchipped them?

When my husband returned to our apartment with coffee, I told him that instead of jogging, I found two dogs worth about as much as our plane flights. I Googled the dog breeds and found they went for upwards of two thousand euros per dog in Sevilla (I'd been transporting over $4000 in USD).

"Where are the dogs?" he asked, handing me my cup.

"It's a long story," I said. "This woman named Cristina took them. She called me a hero."

"Really?" he asked, knowing my struggle with Spanish women. "Good job. Sit down with your café con leche and start at the beginning."

"Is the coffee tosta'o y cola'o?"

"Exactamundo," he said, taking a seat beside me. The clouds started to open and my appetite came back as I thought, maybe I did do the right thing.

FIFTEEN

Up A Tree

LAVERN SPENCER MCCARTHY

I am awakened when the moon is low
by Kitty in the sycamore. Her fright,
expressed in howls, informs me I must go,
still half asleep, to aid her helpless plight.
I climb, but when I reach my naughty pet
she darts away, then clambers down, escapes
into the berry bushes. I regret
I ever came up here where cuts and scrapes
have almost maimed. That limb is out of reach.
I snag my gown on unrelenting wood.
My hair is caught on twigs. I want to screech
for help across the sleeping neighborhood.

The cat is safe, but who will rescue me?
Tomorrow I may still be in this tree.

SIXTEEN

Marry a Cat Man

MCKEL JENSEN

"How many cats have you had?" I asked as I stood looking across my date's backyard.

I had never dated a man that had cats before, and at the time I was stuck with this stereotypical idea that only single women liked them.

"Well," Daniel said. "Let's see, there was Puma—he was my favorite. Then there were the two cats that my friend had me take care of and he never came back for. Then Mojo and Jinxy." He paused to count with his fingers. "What is that? Five? Maybe I've had five. I've lost count."

"Have you ever had a dog?" I asked.

"Yeah, we had Bootsy. He's buried somewhere behind the shed." He pointed to the shed at the far end of the property.

Note to self: if I marry this man and move to this house, tread lightly with my shovel when doing improvements in the yard.

"How many pets have you had?" Daniel turned the question to me.

I confessed that I didn't need my fingers to count the number of pets I'd had in my three decades of life. If I didn't count the fish I had for a week when I was ten, or the black widow spider I put in a jar and took to my junior high school to show everyone, the grand total of was zero. None. My mom said that we traveled too much for pets. However, I have seen my mom flinch at the site of fur or feathers more times than I have fingers to count.

So, at the age of 32, when I said "I do" to my husband Daniel, I was also saying "I do" to his cats.

I have to say, dating Daniel was a special kind of adventure. We met online before dating apps were a thing. We both lived in Northern Utah communities that didn't have a strong single scene and both of us found each other shortly after signing up for services.

Now you need to know, dating sites have their issues and it quickly became apparent that humor does not translate very well. When I first signed up, I saw one man posing with his grandma who was clearly dying in a hospital bed (weird), while another man had actual professional pictures taken of him and his cat (also weird). Other candidates included about fifteen million guys that took selfies in front of the bathroom mirror.

Personally, my friends tried to persuade me to not post a picture of me holding an ice cream cone.

"You don't want a guy to think you eat too much," they said.

Please note, I was not overweight and I wondered why on earth would a guy would find holding an ice cream cone as a turn off. Do single women not eat? Maybe they don't eat ice cream? Or is it just socially incorrect to advertise that we eat? Well, I ate an ice cream cone while on a cruise and someone took my pictures, that's what I had.

A few days into scrolling for potential dates, a new picture popped up. Black and white portrait of a thirty-year-old man in a flat front cap. Handsome. As I explored his page, I saw more pictures of him and learned he had just run the Salt Lake City half marathon. Bingo. I was interested.

"Hi," I posted. "Do you like to run? I'm about to run a 10K."

He responded quickly and we started chatting through the website. I sincerely believe that you can't get to know someone very well through text messages, or even through phone conversations, so after a few short calls we made plans to meet. He was funny, very handsome, I felt comfortable with him, and we started dating—like for real.

A few short weeks into this budding relationship I took the thirty-minute drive from my home near Ogden to his home in Brigham City to see him. I had made the drive several times by now but I still didn't know what to do with his cats when I got there.

"Why are you sitting over there?" he asked. I had found myself on the far end of the couch.

"Well, Mojo is sitting there." I pointed to the cat in the prime seat.

"Then move him."

"You can do that?" It honestly didn't occur to me that I could take away the autonomy of a cat.

"Yeah," he said. I watched as Daniel walked over and pushed the cat onto the floor. "He's a cat."

"Huh." I sighed. "How old is Mojo?"

The cat was scary to look at. Almost black, his fur barely hiding the bones beneath, and his green eyes sunken so deep he reminded me that age was not a number, it was a condition. And that condition brought with it a very grumpy vibe.

"I think he's eighteen." Daniel sat down next to me with his laptop. "Look, I still have access to our dating profiles. Look at this."

He pulled up his profile, and I made fun of him for his stupid bio.

I like things and stuff. That's literally all that it said in his bio.

Here I had been worried about a picture of me holding an ice cream cone and articulating everything about myself in a paragraph, and all he included was *I like things and stuff.* Clearly, men and women worry about very different things. We then spent the next thirty minutes comparing our profiles and laughing at all the half-truths that we posted to look better to potential mates.

His long-haired, orange, nutter-butter of a cat wove through my feet then jumped up on the couch and settled in next to Daniel for a scratch.

"I love this cat," he said. "Jinxy has helped me through my mom's passing. I can't imagine living without this cat."

Dan's fondness for Jinxy was clear, but as my nose

started to itch, a twinge of worry escaped that he might have to decide between me or the cat. If allergies got in the way of this romance, would I have to tell him to get rid of the cat?

"Did I ever show you these pictures?" Daniel interrupted my thought as he worked his way through folders on his laptop. "I had my friend who is a photographer take professional pictures of me with Jinxy."

At the time the pictures were taken, Jinxy looked ridiculous. Because of his matted hair, he had to be shaved down and Daniel opted for the "lion's mane package" at the local groomers. Jinxy had all the hair surrounding his face, a pom-pom at the end of his tail, and something akin to Ugg boots above each paw. It was ridiculous, but it was cute. In one picture, Jinxy looked excitedly off in a direction off camera while Daniel, in a 1970s, western frill cream and brown jacket with snap buttons, matched his off-screen stare with enthusiasm.

"You have no idea what it's like to take a picture with a cat," Daniel said. It's true, I did not. I had absolutely no idea. "It wasn't like I was expecting at all. You have to follow the cat's lead. The cat will never do what you want it to do, so you have to follow the cat."

It was after he showed me a few more that it slowly started to dawn on me. "I've seen these before. You're the guy that posted pictures of himself with his cat!"

Daniel smiled. "Yeah. I thought it was funny when I put them up on my dating profile, but then realized I would never get a date."

He was right. If I knew he was the guy with the cat pictures, I wouldn't have gone out with him. Yet here I was, on his couch, laughing at cat pictures and wanting to make out with him.

Months later, I married that cat lover and, by marriage, I was now the caregiver of two cats: Mojo and Jinxy. I learned how to care for cats and actually enjoyed having their company when Daniel was at work. Allergies weren't the problem I thought they would be, and I was able to prove dominance when Jinxy took the good spot on the couch. (Mojo, the old sack of bones, could sit where he wanted. I was certain those decrepit eyes could summon demons from Hades if I even tried. He had surprisingly quick reflexes for his age.) I was getting the hang of taking care of things, but was thankful that Daniel always cleaned the litterbox and took care of any "gifts" Jinxy brought into the home.

One day after I had settled into my new home, I don't remember why, but I had to move the beloved Jinxy cat in all her fluff to a different room.

"What are you doing?" Daniel asked.

"What do you mean?"

"Look at your arms." I had the cat in my hands with my arms completely outstretched. The cat was dangling from his –uh, armpits as if he were a baby with a poopy diaper.

"Well, I'm still new at this. Leave me alone." Both of us laughed.

I had a baby with that cat lover. Three babies, in fact, though not all at once. When I was pregnant with our first, we noticed that Mojo looked more like death than ever before. When he started peeing in places he shouldn't, and looking like he was hating life more than living it, we had to make the decision to put him down.

I never liked that cat. He was mean, old, moody, uncomfortable to look at and would box at your legs if you dared walk too closely to him, but I cried like I lost my best friend when the vet put him down.

"Will he forgive us?" I asked Daniel, feeling like most of the questions regarding the death of a pet should have been asked when I was in fifth grade.

"When I lost my first pet, my dad told me that you can choose two pet to take with you to heaven." Daniel always looked to his dad's wisdom for things like this.

"Is Mojo one of those two?" I asked in between sobs.

"Um. No."

"Hum. Poor Mojo."

"The vet said we did the right thing," he said. "He told me Mojo's kidneys were failing, that's why he was peeing where he shouldn't."

I couldn't get myself to go in the room where Mojo took his last breath. While the vet performed the procedure, I sat in the waiting room blaming hormones for all my tears and watched other pet owners leave with living pets. *Damn cat*, I thought to myself.

The woman next to me eyed my round belly and said, "Animals have a way of getting into our hearts."

After that day, Jinxy ruled the house as the only cat. He

sat large on the sofa and got treated with food dropped from the counter as he weaved between our legs. Daniel also smothered him with affection and extra cans of wet food. Jinxy was pretty happy.

Then the baby came.

One day soon after, Jinxy just disappeared. He was always an indoor/outdoor cat and would roam our area of town, but he always came home.

"Do you think he died?" I asked Dan softly.

"Maybe," he said. "Animals have a tendency to hide with they are dying. He probably crawled in the irrigation ditch passed away."

I thought of the time we were headed out of town for Christmas. This was before Mojo died and we were trying to get the cats inside so we could lock them in the house while we were away. We couldn't find Jinxy, but we believed he was somewhere close. That day, we decided to hand out our remaining Christmas gifts to our neighbors, and as the old lady with dementia next door greeted us, we could see down her hallway all the way to the closed-in porch, and there, minding his business, was Jinxy.

"What do we say?" I asked Daniel. "'Hey, our cat is in your house, can we have him back?'"

We laughed about the predicament and knew he would be a free cat soon, but probably not before we needed to leave. Luckily, Dan's brother lived close and went over to our house that night to let Jinxy in.

This time was different, though. Jinxy had been missing days, then for a couple weeks. At the time we didn't know he would return two months later, well fed, groomed and ready to get the H.E.-double-hockey-sticks out of our baby-filled home and back with his other family. So, we kept tabs on the animal shelter hoping to find our missing cat, yet no cat matched his description. However, by checking in on the shelter, we learned of the little grey, two-week-old kitten with blue eyes that had come in. Maybe this kitten could fill the cat-sized whole in our hearts.

It was Halloween day when we went to the animal shelter to meet this grey kitty. Daniel was so excited. She was really small, just a few weeks old, and light grey. This tiny thing had the brightest blue eyes with dark slits down the middle. She had us at me-ow.

The woman at the shelter told us the story of how they acquired this little girl. Apparently, she was born in a wall and the renters of the place heard meowing. When they investigated, they found the mom, a brother and this little girl. The other litter mates had died, and soon the brother died too. So, this girl was the only remaining littermate. The woman told us they couldn't do an adoption that day, but asked if we could watch the kitten overnight for them, as it was Halloween. She would stop by in a few hours with the cat, if that was alright. To this day, part of me wonders if the reason she waited was to make sure we were the right fit and then I laugh when she arrived and saw a metal statue of a cat holding a welcome sign on the front door and our cat-themed doormat. She also saw the kid-like expression on Daniel's face when he answered the door.

"Check in with us tomorrow and we will see what we can do," she said. She had a kid with her that looked anxious to get trick-or-treating.

As soon as the door closed, we let the cat climb all over us. She meowed loudly as she adjusted to new people.

I never had pets growing up, but for about two years of my childhood, I kept of list of names for a time when I would have a pet. Most of the names were intended for animals like giraffes or penguins, but I had a few for dogs and cats. I had no idea if that list still exists or where to even look, but my dream of naming a pet was in reach.

"What's your process for naming a pet?" I asked Dan. All my questions seemed so childish because I was experiencing pets for the first time.

"You just start calling it different things until one sticks."

I yearned to be the one that came up with a name that stuck, but I had competition with someone that has had multiple pets his whole life.

"How did you choose Jinxy's name? Or Mojos?"

"Jinxy was the name of the cat in *Meet the Parents*," he said. "And Mojo came to my house as Mojo. I didn't name him."

We pulled out a notebook and started to jot down ideas. I didn't want anything too *on-the-nose*, like directly out of movie, or too common. I have since met cats with no names, but I name them for their owner anyway. How can you have a cat without a name?

I don't remember the other names we considered, but somehow the name Calibri stuck. *Calibri*. Like the font. Because I am a writer. I thought it was clever and I had recently seen *Runaway Bride* where Richard Gere had a cat named Italics. No one would ever see the connection!

"What did you name your cat?" A woman down the street learned we had adopted a cat.

"Calibri," I answered.

"Ah, like in *Runaway Bride*."

Note to self, maybe I'm not as subtle as I think I am. But at least we chose Calibri instead of Times New Roman.

I loved the fact that we got our kitty on Halloween. We had our three-month old baby dressed up as a cat until he managed to pull everything off of him and preferred to hangout in his onesie. But for festivity's sake, Daniel and I wanted to play the part, too, so we got out some cat ears, drew triangle noses and whiskers on our faces. My husband was a good sport and allowed me to add rosy cheeks to his ensemble to enhance the whiskers. One of my most treasured pictures is the three of us, pulling fierce cat faces into the camera with our new kitty on Daniel's shoulder. At first glance, if you weren't paying attention, you would certainly miss the cat. But it was certainly Facebook worthy and got a lot of likes.

A few trick-or-treaters stopped by before Daniel realized we didn't have any kitty food.

"I'm going to run to Walmart." He grabbed the keys from the piano and headed out. I manned the house, baby in one arm, kitten in my hand.

A short time passed before he came home.

"I got everything!" he said, pulling out all the kitty supplies from the grey plastic bag.

"Um, Dan?" I couldn't stop looking at his face. He couldn't stop telling me about his purchases. I tried again. "Dan," I said.

He looked up at me. "What?"

"Go look in the mirror." I watched as he walked to the mirror in our living room and stifled a laugh as he reached up to the whiskers drawn on earlier with my eyeliner.

"Well, that explains a lot."

"What explains a lot?" I asked.

He started to giggle.

"I got to the check stand with all our supplies and told the cashier, 'We got a kitty today!' and she just looked at me. She didn't say anything."

Both of us started to giggle at the thought of a man with whiskers and rosy cheeks in his 30s buying kitty supplies, and excitedly exclaiming to anyone listening that he got a kitty today!

"Oh, I wish I was there to see this." At this point I was wiping tears off my cheeks, careful not to wipe off my own whiskers.

"I don't know what's worse," Daniel said catching his breath. "I remembered to take my cat ears off. Would it had been better if I had them on?"

"Well, it is Halloween," I reassured him.

"By the look on the cashier's face, I don't think it mattered."

That night as we tucked our feet under the blankets on our bed, we watched Calibri jump from my toes to Daniel's toes, and I'd watch Daniel laugh.

"I think I might like having a cat," I said.

Truthfully, I wasn't bonding with the cat, but I was bonding with the man that loved having this cat.

After over a decade of marriage, my advice: If you want a good laugh, and someone that loves hard, is inquisitive and excited about little furry things in life, marry a cat man, even if it's weird at first.

SEVENTEEN

The Marrow of the Matter

FELICIA ROSE

Six months after I retired from my job as a university librarian, my psychiatrist advised me to get a dog. "I don't like dogs," I said.

"Perhaps you'll learn to." She jotted the word "dog" on a script and handed it to me. Her familiar soft brown eyes, salt-and-pepper hair, and silvery voice offered a modicum of comfort.

"Somehow, I doubt it."

"Look, George, I've known you for seven years. You've tried hypnosis, meditation, and yoga. Why not try a dog?"

I adjusted my tie and smoothed a crease in my vest. "Imagine dog hairs on the Oriental rug," I said. "Or, heaven forbid, piddle on the hardwood floors."

"You're an active man, George. If I up your medication, you'll spend your retirement snoozing in an armchair. You know I seldom give advice. But now here it is. Take that script, and get a dog."

After the session, I walked up Madison to Eighty-First and then turned east. It was a brilliant winter day, and tidy, white-haired ladies walked miniature poodles with matching white fur. A man wearing a bow tie and a houndstooth suit strolled along Third. His Scottish terrier wore a Glen plaid coat. Both the man and the dog boasted a calm, self-contained mien.

At home, I brewed a cup of Viennese coffee and drank it over the *Times*. An article in the Science section discussed the side effects of a certain medication. I'd never heard of the drug. Still, it made me worry about my own prescriptions. I breathed deeply to calm my nerves. Then I went to the kitchen to wash the cup.

I retained privileges at the university library, so the next day I headed downtown to search for reading material. Two canine-themed books caught my eye. I borrowed them and then continued my walk. Along the way, I imagined owning a Scottish terrier, black and sleek, like the one I'd seen. But though fit, I verged on stout; walking a petite dog would have highlighted my girth. A dog park on the way roused me from my thoughts. Eight or ten motley hounds barked and ran and peed. Their owners, dressed in sundry versions of grunge, tossed soggy tennis balls to their charges. One young man used newspaper to dispose of his dog's waste. As he carried the parcel to the refuse bin, the contents fell on his shoe.

"No," I said to the psychiatrist the following week. "A dog is out of the question. The next thing you know, I'll be living in a mud-sloshed dive."

"Really, George. Must everything be a slippery slope?"

"Karen, you know very well I can't even live with another *human being*. Remember what I told you about my college roommate who put his shoes on the bed?"

"Look, it's your life, George. But maybe a dog'll contribute to your peace of mind without the side effects of all those meds."

I fingered the chain on my pocket watch and smoothed out the kinks. "Perhaps," I said.

That night, I sat in my armchair and perused the books. Several breeds drew my attention. I especially liked the ones depicted in Renaissance art; they, along with their masters, appeared well-groomed and staunch. I put my feet on the ottoman and removed a piece of lint from my robe. A dog might be lying beside me just now. A mastiff seemed a solid choice. But it required more space than a one-bedroom apartment afforded. A basset hound sounded appealing for its size. But it slobbered and howled. I read on. Apparently, Freud had a chow. The photo before me depicted the analyst hunched in his chair, his arm round his pet. His three-piece suit appeared impeccable. So did his office.

Still, to be on the safe side, the following day, I increased my service with Heavenly Maids. Then I searched for a dog. A week later, I brought home a chow.

For the first five minutes, Jofi stood in the hallway on the hardwood floor and stared at a piece of lint. So as not to disturb her, I laid my overcoat on the armchair and stared as well. When the mantel clock struck twelve, I said, "Jofi, would you like some lunch?" She ignored me. Finally, I had no choice but to remove the object of her attention and place it in the trash. She looked at me with soft brown eyes. I imagined I saw a thanks.

According to the lady at the kennel, Jofi had been a surrender dog. The previous owner, an elderly man, could no longer attend her. "It's not easy in the city," she'd said. "You know, having to walk them two or three times a day. That poor man didn't even have an elevator. He had to take her up and down four flights of stairs morning, noon, and night."

"I'm in fine fettle," I said. I meant it in a physical sense. She nodded and handed me the leash.

After lunch, Jofi and I walked along Museum Mile. I felt dapper in my tweed overcoat and flat cap with Jofi by my side. Several poodles approached to sniff her, and the white-haired ladies nodded faintly and then, unsmiling, looked away.

As we turned down Second, Jofi and I passed the man with the Scottish terrier. His dark wool pants fit his sturdy figure well, even when he bent to clean up after his dog, which he did with aplomb.

When Jofi and I returned to the apartment, I removed my shoes and Jofi spent a good ten minutes cleaning her paws. She licked them meticulously, producing a sound akin to that of sucking on a marrow-filled bone. Then, she jumped on the armchair. My heart raced, and I yelled at her to get down. She did so but then went to the corner to sulk. Feeling despondent about the matter, I invited her to sit beside me on the sofa. She laid her head on my lap, and I petted her as I read.

The radiator in the psychiatrist's office blasted steam, fogging the window and all but concealing the air shaft on the other side. I unfolded my handkerchief and wiped my brow. "Karen," I said, "I wonder if this is cause for concern."

"So, George, if I understand correctly, you're concerned about not being concerned."

"Precisely. If I don't mind Jofi on the sofa—if, in fact, I invite her to be on the sofa—then the next thing you know, I'll not care if people wear shoes in the apartment. Or, for that matter, put them on the bed."

"And so?"

"And so my material life will be as disordered as my inner life."

"Might Jofi be making your inner life more serene?"

One bright spring morning, Jofi sat by the door and wagged her tail. I placed my empty coffee cup in the sink and got the leash. We strolled along the East River Promenade watching joggers and boats. When I sat on a bench, Jofi hunched beside me and placed her paw around my leg. I took out a book and read. On the way home, we saw the man with the Scottish terrier headed in our direction. This time we nodded. Jofi gamboled in delight.

. . .

It rained heavily for the next four days, and so Jofi and I limited our walks to within a block of the building. White poodles abounded in raincoats and booties, but the white-haired ladies made themselves scarce. Instead, at the other end of the leashes were maids in black dresses with white aprons and trim. Jofi did her business but then tugged on the leash toward the building. When we entered, she wiped her paws on the mat.

I thought of the man with the Scottish terrier but did not see him again until the following Friday when the rain cleared and Jofi and I ventured east. He had just finished curbing his dog and was now headed west. The two beasts pulled us toward one another. I breathed deeply and then spoke. "I appreciate your doing your share to keep our city clean."

"It's rather inconsiderate that some people don't." He had a plangent voice, which contrasted with self-assured eyes. We continued our discussion of tidiness and dogs before proceeding to other matters. By the time we'd circled Conservatory Garden, I'd learned, among other details, that Lucian worked as a book editor specializing in Renaissance art.

"Well, George," the psychiatrist said. "It's been, what, a year now since you got Jofi? Eight months since Lucian came into your life? You were my first client in New York, and now you're my last. I trust you'll continue to function reasonably, which is to say within the normal range of neuroses. As for myself, I plan to retire."

A month later, we had our final session. As a gift of appreciation, I gave her a photograph of Jofi savoring a bone on the Oriental rug. She gave me a set of bookends. We thanked one another, and I removed a handkerchief from my pocket to dab my eyes.

When I opened the apartment door, Jofi greeted me with a wag of her tail. I placed the bookends, two bronze canines, on the mantel beside the clock. Lucian suggested we name them after our dogs. So now the bronze versions of Brigitte and Jofi stand neatly on the bookshelf securing our canine-themed books.

As for the actual terrier and chow, evenings they sit on either end of the sofa while Lucian and I relax between them and read.

Originally published in *The Westchester Review* (fall 2020) with the title "Jofi."

About the Authors

Sherrie Gavin is a PhD candidate at the University of New England researching Latter-day Saint Food Studies. Her books include *Baptism & Boomerangs* and the forthcoming *Adaeze Reads the Bible* and *Turning Pink*. Her writing has appeared in *The Friend, Meridian Magazine, Exponent II*, and her favourite, The Writer's Cache. She spends her time between the US and Australia with her husband, two daughters, and their fluffy fur-baby, Luna.

Fawn Groves has served for over 30 years in a variety of education-focused roles. These have included teaching mathematics and ESL in secondary public schools, serving on the faculty of Utah State University's School of Teacher Education and Leadership, supporting USU's diverse student and scholar populations as an advisor and administrator, and serving on the Executive Board of Utah's chapter of the National Association for Multicultural Education.

Once **Dianne Hardy** retired as a music professor, she began her writing career. Her memoir *For Cryin' Out Loud!* and many of her short stories have won awards, including her story about her cat, Aura. She has three children and several grandchildren and lives in Utah.

McKel Jensen's work has appeared in multiple anthologies including the award-winning *In Spite of the Dark*. Her story "The Weeping Willow at Goblin Creek" won a Woolley award and appeared in the anthologies *Soul, Sand, & Sky* as well as *Utah's Best Poetry and Prose 2022*. McKel earned her Master of Arts degree from Weber State University and currently resides in Brigham City, Utah with her cat man, three kids, one cat, and a dog.

Tim Keller is an avid reader who also has a weak spot for animals. He likes traveling, 80's music, and if the highway patrol is to be believed, driving way too fast. After working as a bouncer, mortgage researcher, computer repair technician, caregiver, and a brief, albeit disastrous, stint as a waiter in anachronistic drag, he decided he wanted to be a writer when he grew up. A keen observer of human nature, Tim enjoys writing stories about all kinds of people from all walks of life. His work can be found in various literary journals and anthologies including *Mirrored Realities, In the Shimmering, Between Places*, and the *Helicon West Anthology*.

LaVern Spencer McCarthy has written and published twelve books of poetry and fiction. Her work has appeared in *Writers and Readers Magazine, Meadowlark Reader, Agape Review, Bards Against Hunger, Down in The Dirt, The Evening Universe, Fresh Words Magazine, Wicked Shadows Press, Midnight Magazine, Pulp Cult Press, Metasteller* and others.

She is a life member of Poetry Society of Texas. A poem she wrote was nominated for the 2023 Push Cart Prize.

With the cognitive revolution came words. By way of words we are not alone. Lady Meow taught me that.
   -An Ancient Sapien, aka **Michael Oborn.**

Edmond A Porter currently resides in Tremonton, Utah. Originally from Preston, Idaho, Edmond has lived in Brazil, Burley, Idaho, and Zillah, Washington. Upon graduation from Utah State University, he worked in the canned food industry for 45 years. Following his retirement in 2019, he and his wife moved to Utah to be closer to family.

Edmond began writing in elementary school, edited his high school newspaper, and wrote budget proposals and technical papers as part of his career.

Now he is retired, he has returned to writing for fun. Published works include two articles in the Utah Quilt Guild Newsletter, over 50 stories on Medium.com, and stories in two anthologies.

Edmond is a member of the League of Utah Writers, participating in the Cache Valley Writers and the Brigham City Writers Chapters. He also participates in a local non-affiliated writing group, The Sapling House Literary Society. He can be found at edmondaporter.com and medium.com@eporter609.

He currently has three WIP novels that still need a lot of work.

Sharolyn Richards is the author of two books, *Arlington's Treasure* and *Betrayed in Taiwan*, with many more on the way. She has a B.A. in Creative Writing from BYU-Idaho and M.S. in Literature and Writing from Utah State University. She loves traveling, taking experiences from that and putting them in her books. When she is not writing or teaching for BUI-Idaho Online, she likes to spend time with her husband and kids, cook yummy food, and have dance parties in the kitchen with her kids. You can find her online at sharolynrichardswriter.com

Felicia Rose's work has appeared in *Mr. Beller's Neighborhood, The Helicon West Anthology, The Sun, The Way to My Heart: An Anthology of Food-Related Romance, Mother Earth News, The Westchester Review,* and elsewhere. She lives in New York.

John Savoie teaches great books at Southern Illinois University Edwardsville. His poems have appeared in *Poetry, Best New Poets,* and *Poetry in Motion*. His first collection *Sehnsucht* has recently won the Prize Americana.

A close friend once told her that she bloomed where she was planted, explaining how hard it was to get **Anne Stark** to leave her home. Nevertheless, her husband managed to pull on those roots, and the two of them left for Spain for a total of a year and a half, traversing the Iberian Peninsula and blogging along the way. Languages, writing, and researching fueled her much-loved career as a lecturer at Utah State, but now she enjoys flipping pancakes for kids and grandkids when she's not writing stories or playing her guitar. To read more of her work, go to *WordPress, Huffington Post,* or read these past anthologies of The Writers' Cache: *'Tis the Season* and *Lost and Found.*

David S. Taylor, aka Banjoman, aka The Music Taylor, also calls himself *The Renaissance Man from Glen Arbor* in his memoir, which chronicles his remarkable experiences as a rocket scientist, missionary, mountaineer, minstrel, and cancer survivor. He earned a BS degree in chemical engineering and an MBA. Since retiring from a career in aerospace, he concentrates on writing creative nonfiction essays for anthologies, like this one, published by the League of Utah Writers. His published works include *Bring-to-Life Book of Mormon Stories: A Reference Guide for Speakers, Teachers, Students, and Parents; E-Z Christmas Songs for 5-String Banjo;* and *Beginning Melody, Harmony, and Rhythm for Folk Guitar.* Early 2025 will see the release of his second *Reference Guide* to the scriptures, *Bring-to-Life Old Testament Stories.* David lives in Hyde Park, Utah with his wife, Kathy. They have four married children, 17 grandchildren, and one great-grandchild so far.

My name is **Woodrow Walters**. I live in Logan, Utah, and have been writing seriously for a little over a year. I was recently made a co-editor of nonfiction with *Sinkhollow*, the undergraduate literary magazine published by students at Utah State University. I write a mixture of fiction and nonfiction, with a focus on the silver linings in the dark moments of life. I hope you enjoy what you read of my work.

E.B. Wheeler is the author of over a dozen books of history, historical fiction, and historical fantasy, including Whitney Award finalists *Born to Treason* and *A Proper Dragon* and Whitney Award winner *Cruel Magic*, as well as several short stories, essays, magazine articles, and scripts for educational software programs. She earned a B.A. in history with an English minor from BYU and graduate degrees in history and landscape architecture from Utah State University. She lives in Utah with her human family and her dog, cat, rabbits, and chickens.

www.ingramcontent.com/pod-product-compliance
Lightning Source LLC
Chambersburg PA
CBHW062008070426
42451CB00008BA/274